Securing Converged IP Networks

Securing

Converged

IP Networks

Tyson Macaulay

CISSP, CISA, ISSPCS
Director
Bell Security Solutions Inc.
Bell Canada

CRC Press
Taylor & Francis Group
Boca Raton London New York

CRC Press is an imprint of the
Taylor & Francis Group, an **informa** business

AN AUERBACH BOOK

CRC Press
Taylor & Francis Group
6000 Broken Sound Parkway NW, Suite 300
Boca Raton, FL 33487-2742

First issued in paperback 2019

ISBN-13: 978-0-8493-7580-4 (hbk)
ISBN-13: 978-0-367-39080-8 (pbk)

Visit the Taylor & Francis Web site at
http://www.taylorandfrancis.com

and the CRC Press Web site at
http://www.crcpress.com

Preface

This book was inspired by the main promoters of Internet Protocol (IP) convergence (product vendors and solutionsproviders) who assume that the security controls and safeguards, which represent the status quo for "data only" Information Technology (IT) networks, will be adequate for the converged Information and Communication Technology (ICT) networks. ICT networks are different because they mingle data assets with assets such as voice, entertainment and media, industrial process controls, metering, physical security, and more. It is the authors' opinion that IP convergence represents both a new business imperative and a fundamentally new security paradigm, one which is not yet commonly discussed. Under IP convergence, the network becomes a far more critical infrastructure component requiring greater awareness and better management. Whereas the loss of assurance in the IT network has previously meant work slow-down and varying degrees of inconvenience, the compromise of the ICT network is coming to mean work stoppage, financial loss, and, very likely, physical perils.

ICT is the term and acronym coming to supplant the tried and true "IT" (Information Technology) acronym, perhaps reflecting a growing awareness around the union of data and other information and communication assets on a single IP network. The differences between information and communication are not necessarily defined in any standard way; the term "information" may be more oriented toward the description of a static, archivable asset while the term "communication" has a more real-time and possibly inter-personal connotation. This distinction will vary from person to person, but most people agree that "ICT" implies a richness of features and functions that "IT" does not.

The on-going shift in market terminology from IT to ICT is important to this book. The shifting terminology is a leading indicator to the conclusive acceleration of IP convergence. The popularization of the ICT acronym also changes things because traditionally IT and "Security" equals "ITS," and lots has been written about ITS. But not a lot has been written about ICT Security and no one (yet) speaks about "ICTS"—it's probably too much of a mouthful? But this goes back to the issue of vendors making assumptions about ICT security. Is it the case that ICTS was really no different IT Security? Perhaps. But initial research prior to committing to write this book indicated that ICTS represented new security and assurance challenges for organizations. Using terminology as a litmus test for an evolving security requirement is clearly not scientific and could be cynically described as opportunistic. But the advent of ICT terminology and its adoption by large organizations/users/media validates it as a concept. This in turn introduces ICT Security as an independent concept worthy of discussion. This book is an attempt to start a larger discussion around how ICT impacts the field of technology security and assurance.

Tyson Macaulay, CISSP, CISA, ISSPCS

Contents

6. What Comes Next? **237**
AUTHOR: *Tyson Macaulay*
CONTRIBUTING AUTHOR: *Lee Wagner*

Contributors

Pritpal Bhogal   Consultant

Tyson Macaulay   Bell Security Solutions, Inc.

George McBride   Lucent Technologies

Phil Norton   A.J. Gallagher & Co.

Robert Prudhomme   InCode Wireless

Lee Wagner   InCode Wireless

Understanding Internet Protocol (IP) Convergence

AUTHOR: **Tyson Macaulay**
Bell Security Solutions, Inc.

INTRODUCTION

Railroads were the industrial kingpins of their day. Railroads dominated industry, generated enormous wealth for their owners, and propelled the growth of nations and empires. The primary industrial inputs to the railroad was a constant and reliable supply of coal and steel; coal to fire the engines and steel to extend and maintain the rails. Today assurance is the coal and steel of the information age and the converged IP world.

Assurance is a single concept that embodies a trinity of Information and Communication Technology (ICT) security requirements: confidentiality, integrity and availability. Confidentiality represents protection from disclosure to unauthorized parties, or the disclosure to nominally authorized parties at the wrong time. Integrity means that data are free from corruptions, changes, or deletions both intentional and accidental. Availability refers to data or systems being up and running as required/anticipated, and also the property of delivering information at necessary speeds and in the correct sequence. Together, these properties represent the sensitivity requirements of a given system, application, process, or data set. Assurance is the degree of confidence an entity has that the properties of confidentiality, integrity and availability are being supported.

Without assurance, convergence of telecommunications onto a single IP carrier is a technical possibility but a business fantasy. Convergence will not be achieved without a comprehensive ability to apply and maintain assurance in the components, applications and data resident and connected to the converged network.

In this first chapter, we will deal with some fundamental concepts around ICT convergence and assurance:

- Who should care about security under ICT convergence and what might it mean to the professional mandates of a relatively wide variety of business roles?
- What is ICT convergence, what are its component parts and how has the eponymous Internet Protocol (IP) come to play the role of both catalyst and glue?
- What is driving ICT convergence from a cost, competition and regulatory perspective, and how do these factors combine in unexpected ways to accelerate convergence?
- This chapter will end with a brief outline of the rest of the book.

Each subsequent chapter will start with its own summary and value-assessment about the relative potential value of a given chapter to a given business role, as they are defined below.

STRIKE ONE MISCONCEPTION

Convergence does not start with Voice over Internet Protocol (VOIP). VOIP is merely a common starting point for organizations starting to experience convergence of their ICT assets. There are many types of ICT assets converging and many organizations may be undergoing convergence without a significant awareness of this fact!

Telephony services—VOIP—is a major, high profile ICT asset but is by no means the only place where the convergence process may commence. The reason that VOIP is so high profile is because the business case for VOIP convergence is relatively simple:

- Savings in Moves, Adds, and Changes (MACs) to telephone devices in large organizations with thousands of phones can top $1 million in just a couple of years.[1]
- A 50% reduction in cabling costs in the new building, and elimination of PSTN trunking for the new sites.
- Increased system resiliency, including the ability to log into a phone at a recovery site.
- Increased productivity because of the mobility of VOIP phones.

More mundane ICT assets and devices may beat telephony services and VOIP to the convergence-punch, and start to appear on the IP network well in advance. Managers need to be acutely aware of this fact because as each asset is converged on the IP network, the sensitivity of the network increases (see Chapter 2).

---

[1] Case studies demonstrate two diverge roads to IP, Telemanagement, March 2005, pg 15.

WHO SHOULD READ THIS BOOK?

This book is intended for those who are concerned about and interested in ICT and the impact of both good and bad assurance on people, processes, technology, and regulatory compliance. Table 1 outlines a variety of potential reader profiles and provides a few bullet points about how this book is applicable to each profile. This profile system will be referred to at the start of each chapter to highlight who is most likely to benefit from a given chapter.

Table 1   Reader Profiles

Role	Interest
CEO/Board Members	• Enterprise risk management - Regulatory compliance impacts of convergence
CFO/COO/Risk Managers	• Enterprise risk management - Liability and insurance costs
CTO/IT Managers and Personnel	• Implementation techniques of converged networks • ROI enhancements around information technology • ICT management practices
CSO/ITS Managers and Personnel	• Controls and safeguards around converged networks • Privacy impacts of converged networks
Auditors	• Sample audit criteria around converged networks
Legislators, Regulators and Government Employees	• Evolving issues reflecting over-riding public interest • Developing regulatory frameworks
Equipment Manufacturers	• Competitive advantage: - New feature sets - Evolving customer demand
Telecom Carriers	• Competitive advantage: - New feature sets - Evolving customer demand
Consultants and Service Providers	• Guidance for provision of new services to organizations - Migrating to converged networks - Threat Risk Assessment services - ERM services
Law Enforcement and Forensics Personnel (Including Forensic Auditors)	• Understanding of evolving cause-and-effect security relationships on converged networks • Investigation techniques and evidentiary material

ASSUMPTIONS

This book is not intended as an ICT security primer for consumption by those looking to become better acquainted with the techniques and technologies associated with ICT. The reader is assumed to already possess an understanding of ICT security principles concerning the Internet and data on Ethernet-based networks. For instance, the reader should have an understanding of the technical and management techniques around people, processes, and technology to provide assurance to systems, applications, and processes. Knowledge—not necessarily extensive but enough to understand basic concepts such as firewalls, security policies, and awareness training—is understood as prerequisite in this book.

This book is for people who need to understand what has changed under convergence.

CONVERGENCE 101

Network convergence in relation to communications technologies has meant a variety of different things over the years, starting with the notion in the late 1980s of one corporate supplier for television and telephony (fixed line and even cellular). However, the idea of mingling these different types of content within the same network "pipe" is a relatively new definition of convergence that was spawned by the advent of Internet Protocol (IP) and the Internet.

The story of IP is really the story of the Internet and is too grand to be (re)told within this book. The most important thing to know about IP is that is has absolutely come to dominate the communications world when it comes to joining network to network to network in a (theoretically) endless, virtual universe of interconnected, sovereign domains. IP is a routing protocol that enables data from one network, for instance an Ethernet network, to be directed to another distant network using either direct or circuitous paths through other intermediate networks. The IP, defined by IETF[2] RFC791 is the routing layer datagram service of the TCP/IP suite. Except ARP and RARP, all protocols within TCP/IP use IP to route frames from host to host. The interconnectedness provided by IP (and supplemented

---

[2] Internet Engineering Task Force; see http://www.ietf.org.

by Transport Communications Protocol—TCP, the primary error-correcting/delivery-assuring mechanism of the Internet) spawned applications like email and file transfers, which were the original "killer apps" that drove Internet growth and adoption starting in the late 1980s. In the early 1990s the World-Wide-Web (WWW) came along as the new killer-app and elevated IP beyond competing data routing standards—such as X.400, for instance. (X.400 is the message transport defined for use between telecommunications vendors and customers by the international consortium of national standards bodies known as ISO. In otherwords, it roughly corresponds to TCP/IP's SMTP and RFC822 header format.) The result was that IP networks, tools, equipment and human skills became widely available and affordable and the IP networks grew even further to absolutely dominate not only inter-domain network communications but intra-domain communications—the office LAN and WAN. Good bye, Banyan. Good bye, Novell. So long, Appletalk. See you later, Token Ring.

But why did convergence take so long in the first place? The reason convergence did not happen earlier in the history of ICT is that there was nothing to converge onto prior to the penetration of broadband (high speed) Internet services to business initially, plus the advent of cheap high-speed access to domestic users. The emergence of IP as the clear and obvious winner of the network-connectedness game in the late 1990s represented a beacon for all the other communications technologies. There was suddenly something to converge toward whether you were running the tried and true SS7 for switched telephony, or tied to an obscure, proprietary vendor protocol for industrial process controls. The business drivers to converge on IP were manifest for organizations of all sizes and consumers, generally:

- Shared physical and logical networks reduce **operational costs**.
- Reduced/commoditized costs introduce new **competitive imperatives** in the market, focused on feature and applications (bells and whistles), and creates . . .
- New **features and functions** to improve productivity and create wider choices for both life-style and work-style.
- New varieties or service impacted the legacy **regulatory environment**.

Taxonomy of Convergence

In many respects the term "IP-world" is a most suitable way to describe the environment of services on IP. Think of email, file transfers, on-line databases and the Web as the initial, primordial soup of communications technology relative to the rapidly evolving "biodiversity" represented by IP convergence.

Convergence is not represented by a mathematically fixed number of applications or technologies. In fact, the number of eligible applications and technologies is forever growing. What follows is a high-level taxonomy of some of converging applications and technologies.

At a high level we will group the converging technologies under the following headings:

- **Triple Play Convergence**: The most obvious, contemporary example of convergence, with data, telephony and entertainment and media services all running on IP. It is relevant to consumers and business.
- **Transparent Convergence**: The movement of communications and control systems to IP from formerly proprietary and stand-alone networks. This convergence is almost entirely unobserved by anyone not closely involved with the management of these communications and control systems, but it has been on-going since the late 1990s and has reached mass-market proportions as of 2006. For example, in Ontario, Canada the primary electricity provider issued an Request for Proposal for IP-based smart meters in March of 2005.[3] The target date for commencing deployment of smart meters was the start of 2006. Transparent convergence is largely relevant to business.
- **Blue Sky Convergence**: The arrival of entirely new, IP-based functionality in existing goods and services, or the creation of entirely new goods and services based upon IP in the imminent future.

---

[3] The RFP issued by Hydro One did not specifically require IP as the network protocol to manage communications between the meter devices and HydroOne WAN; however, TCP/IP was designated as the transport for all meter information within the WAN. Furthermore, while IP was not strictly specified for the meter interface, all the specified layer 1 and 2 carriers are well known as IP carriers; for instance, 1XRTT, WiMAX and 802.11a/b/g.

Name	Definition	Legacy Medium
Triple Play		
Data services	This is the IP-world baseline: email, file transfers, web and web services.	Novell, Banyan, Token Ring, sneaker-net (i.e., passing data around on floppy disks)
Voice telephone	Voice telephony is packetized and placed onto routed IP networks. Voice mail systems are placed on the IP networks and calls may come and go from the Internet or out through gateways designed to interface with the traditional PSTN (Public Switched Telephone Network).	Analogue encoding, switched and dedicated networks
Entertainment and media	Television channels and enhanced services—like pay per view, movie or music downloads—delivered both on a scheduled and on-demand basis.	Radio/wireless signals, analogue signals over coaxial cable, CD ROMs
Transparent		
Physical security	Physical access controls on doors, CCTV for internal and perimeter surveillance, fire alarms and smoke detectors, motion detectors for burglar alarms, public address and intercom systems.	Dedicated, analogue networks, proprietary systems
Supervisor control and Data Acquisition (SCADA)	Remote monitoring and control of manufacturing automation elements such as pumps, temperature gauges, pressure levels	Dedicated, analogue networks, proprietary systems
Banking services	Point-of-sale (POS) and Automated Banking Machines (ABM) for doing credit, debit transactions with merchants, money transfers—and simply obtaining cash	Dedicated, proprietary networks

Facilities management	Monitoring of facilities infrastructure for rapid maintenance, inventory management and efficiencies. Control of heating and cooling systems, water systems, and electrical systems, and eventually IP addresses and simple diagnostic/remote control capabilities applied to light blubs and switches in buildings and perhaps fuel tanks and tires on fleet vehicles.	Dedicated, proprietary networks
Metering	Monitoring of energy, water, parking spaces, and other consumables with faster, more efficient, and more accurate billing and trouble shooting.	Close-range wireless without network
Blue Sky		
Smart durables	Normal appliances like hot water tanks, fridges, stoves, microwaves, televisions, garage door-openers, etc. are embedded with simple network interfaces to embedded systems for the purposes of in-field flaw remediation, license/warranty management, and remote control.	RFID and barcode for logistics without any network
Tele-presence	The ability for people to (physically) engage in localized activities from remote locations; for instance, medical examinations or operations	Robotics on closed networks

THE CONVERGENCE MARKET

To possess a high-level understanding of what technologies IP convergence is composed of, the questions of "when?" and "how much?" must be addressed in order to gauge the imminence and severity of the issues covered by this book. Do we really need to deal with the topic of security and convergence now?

VOIP represents the converged technology with the earliest impact of significant scope and scale. VOIP is the means of converting analogue sounds into digitial packets for transmission over IP networks. 2004 marked the year when significant numbers of consumers started to adopt VOIP. VOIP is projected to reach between 6% and 8% of all broadband consumers by 2009.[4] For large organizations, 2008 is the earliest projected date at which they will start to move in significant numbers to VOIP services and equipment.[5] Similarly, entertainment and media applications like IPTV, movies, and music is projected to start obtaining significant market shares and become a significant revenue business after 2008.[6] Entertainment and media products and services available over converged networks represents the final conversion of traditionally analogue products and services to an end-to-end digital environment—delivered in packetized formats and transported to consumers over broadband Internet connections. VOIP and entertainment and media in combination with data services represent the "triple play" for telecoms companies, which is seen as the current means to market victory.

Paralleling the growth of the high-profile triple-play convergence technologies are the more transparent technologies around Physical Security, Supervisor Controls and Data Acquisition (SCADA) systems, financial transactions, metering and facilities management. Industries using these technologies are seeing a large re-deployment or upgrade of infrastructure components toward IP-based communications and transports.

In the case of Physical Security, "digital video surveillance" is the latest growth industry, with digital cameras replacing analogue cameras in some cases, but in many cases it is a matter of retaining the older, higher-resolution analogue technology and converting the

---

[4] Residential VOIP Analysis, Parks Associates, 2005–06–06.
[5] From VOIP to XOIP, IDC Research, March 2005.
[6] The Business Case for IPTV, Ovum Research, Sept 2004.

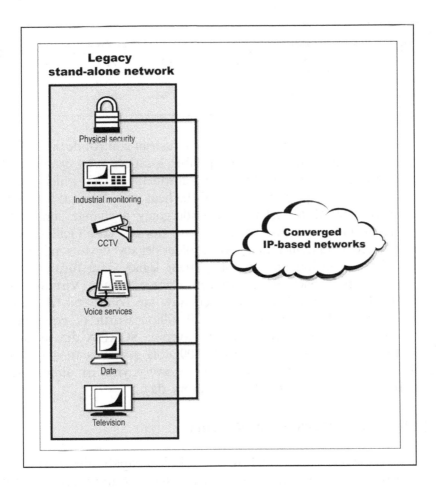

information into digital formats and transporting it over IP networks to centralized digital video management systems. Similarly, the amalgamation of different varieties of physical security controls are on the verge of rapid convergence. This is being seen in the migration of all physical security and access control devices to IP communications: CCTV, intercom, door strikes, guard-station controls, fire and smoke detectors. The market for this type of convergence technology is projected to grow 500% from 2003 to 2007 and have a market value of over $7 billion[7] in North America and over $14 billion world wide.

---

[7] Global Digital Video Surveillance Models, Data Monitor, July 2004.

Forecasted Spending on Converged Physical/Logical Security Projects (US$ Millions)[8]					
	2005	2006	2007	2008	CAGR
North America	691	1713	3707	7039	79%
Europe	572	1220	2751	5186	74%

SCADA systems are made up of industrial control devices often operating in very remote or inhospitable locations. An example of such devices are programmable logic controllers (PLCs), which might control valves on pipelines or control the heat and chemical mixtures in refineries. SCADA systems are undergoing a change similar to Physical Security systems, whereby new devices and facilities will use IP-based communications, while older legacy devices might be fitted with conversion units to place their legacy data formats into IP for transport back to centralized storage points. Virtually all new SCADA systems being deployed now are converged, IP-based technologies and amount to over $20 billion worth of equipment per year world-wide.[9] Given that the average SCADA device (such as a PLC[10] or DCS[11]) may cost $5000, this amounts to 4 million IP-based SCADA devices going on-line every year or almost 450 new IP-based devices every hour of every day.

THE BUSINESS DRIVERS OF CONVERGENCE

While convergence is enabled by the technical capabilities of IP, it is driven by a complex combination of market and non-market forces (demand and supply-side controls). Convergence is a matter of costs, competition, and regulatory legacy. Organizations need to offer goods and services to clients in a way that is better, faster, and cheaper than the competition. Regulatory drivers are inadvertent, and reflect market distortions introduced by government regulation that actually propel convergence in unplanned ways.

---

[8] Trends 2005: Security Convergence Gets Real, Forrester Research, Steve Hunt, Jan 2005.

[9] ARC Group, PLC World Wide Outlook brochure; http://www.arcweb.com/research/pdfs/Study_plc_ww.pdf.

[10] Programmable Logic Controller.

[11] Distributed Control System.

COST DRIVERS

1. The first cost driver is *reducing costs associated with network management.* Total cost of ownership is reduced through:

   - Shared infrastructure—one physical network to maintain and aromatize.
   - Reduced staff and support costs for a common technology and network.
   - Reduced costs associated with Moves, Adds and Changes (MACs) of telephones, specifically in the case of VOIP.[12]
   - Reduced tolls and tariffs associated with intra-office calling, specifically in the case of VOIP.

2. The second cost driver is *capturing of new revenue streams* through new business models, especially in the area of entertainment and media where IP convergence is revolutionizing distribution and marketing for producers of content. Suddenly the old distribution and marketing channels of hard-copy VHS, CDs, or scheduled television with interruptive advertising is no longer the only way to reach consumers. Not only that, but IP-based distribution and marketing tools also make old cost-centers like television advertising increasingly less efficient and effective and provide revenue opportunities to those entities adopting converged technologies.[13]

3. The third cost driver is *increased productivity and efficiency* within the user community by taking advantage of the newest features available for telephony or video. Gains can be realized through:

   - Desktops and phone numbers that roam with the user—no matter where they are in the world.
   - New "presence" applications associated with VOIP telephony, which allow for targeted communications and less time spent "hunting" for individuals.
   - The amalgamation of voice mail, email, and fax to a single desktop interface.

---

[12] Case Studies Demonstrate Two Diverge Roads to IP, Telemanagement, March 2005, pg 15.

[13] Daryl Dunbar, British Telecom, New York presentation, July 21, 2005.

4. The fourth cost driver is *better control of capital.* Convergence allows organizations to have a single management interface to the technologies engaged in the manipulation of corporate information and assets (data, phone calls, media consumption, and provision), generating positive impacts in the area of Enterprise Risk Management:

   - Reduced operational risks associated with control of intellectual property (technology, strategic/tactical market data), production processes, and communications.
   - Reduced financial risks associated with the control of sensitive regulatory (or regulated) data and the assurance of customer, partner, and internal data.

5. The fifth cost driver is *client pull.* Device vendors in both the Triple Play and Transparent world are being forced to meet client demands for IP-based products. "The most significant change has been the evolving customer requirement for open architectures and commercial technology. Our customers wanted the flexibility to buy equipment from any automation supplier and have that equipment work in the multi-vendor environments that exist in most factories." [14]

6. The sixth cost driver is *business continuity and disaster recovery.* The start of the 21st century has seen event after event that highlight the requirements for good business continuity (BC) and disaster recovery (DR) capabilities. But good BC and DR is expensive. Convergence offers the ability to reduce the costs associated with DR and BC due to the ability of IP-based applications, systems, processes and assets to be re-routed/re-directed around failed network segments or facilities. Standard and highly reliable systems like Open Shortest Path First (OSPF) and Border Gateway Protocol (BGP) offer the ability to automatically detect and re-route IP information to secondary sites (DR sites) where back-up components can seamlessly assume the technical capabilities of information assets at costs far more affordable than previously possible. The net result is that the development and support of high-availability capability and assurance for critical converged assets is attainable to more organizations and at lower

---

[14] Rockwell Automation Annual Report, 2004, pg 8.

thresholds. The cost of the safeguard relative to the loses associated with the risk (the impact) have shifted and managers need to be aware of this shift. Managers need to re-visit the costs associated with high-availability under convergence and consider whether the cost of this type of assurance is still out of proportion to the potential loses/impacts. Failure to do so may produce uncomfortable questions from regulators and/or board members during the post-mortem associated with an outage.

The cost drivers for Blue Sky convergence are speculatory and out of scope for this book, which is focused on the present and immediate future. Blue Sky convergence relies upon technology that is merely at the research stage. Unlike Triple Play and Transparent convergence, Blue Sky convergence appears to be driven by several requirements:

1. To deliver services better and faster from remote locations in order to increase competitive advantage or simply shorten the amortization of expensive capital assets (whether they be software programs, super computers or surgeons)
2. To allow for scarce or expensive resources (such as service-engineers, judges, or doctors) to be utilized as much as possible by eliminating "downtime" associated with travel and set-up/tear-down operations.

Blue Sky convergence is seeking the same business outcomes as Triple Play and Transparent convergence, but it goes one step further; it is seeking entirely new production and delivery paradigms. To end users, a phone is a phone; the same for television, security cameras, SCADA information, or water meters. Blue Sky convergence not only engenders a new delivery process but also an entirely new experience for the producer and consumer of the goods and services. In fact, Blue Sky convergence really has little to do with convergence per se because an IP transport will be assumed by the implementers as a matter of the delivery ethos.

COMPETITIVE DRIVERS

The Triple Play form of convergence is essentially about one thing—retaining or gaining customers: "... bundling has become more than a marketing tool; it is a necessary strategy for service providers to achieve three key objectives: acquire new customers, charge their current customers more, and retain their current customers." [15] Triple Play bundles also serve to actually reduce customer churn because customers are less likely to jump to a "better offer" the more comprehensively engaged they are with a supplier. This is a critical consideration for Triple Play providers; converged-services such as VOIP and entertainment and media must be deployed as soon as possible in a highly competitive market place.

---

[15] Bundles: Beyond the Triple Play, RHK Insight, November 2004.

REGULATORY DRIVERS

Regulatory drivers of convergence are diferent from cost and competitive drivers because they are "economic-push"/supply-side drivers, and therefore not market driven.

In most parts of the world, with the current exceptions of Canada and Singapore, Triple Play is very lightly regulated because IP convergence is perceived to have supplied a level competitive field. If Internet/data is available over IP, then just about any provider can deliver VOIP and entertainment and media services. In the case of VOIP, market entry for a service-provider wannabes has even been calculated at less than $10,000![16] The provision of the network and the value-added services are distinct. Since there are no competitive advantages around network ownership, regulatory requirements for Triple Play services are less obvious.

Regulation is intended to provide a balance between public interests and private interests and motives. This has always been the stated intent of regulation in the telecommunications industry, however, there are regulatory elements in most national regimes that enable regulated service providers to assertively push converged services onto clients. This phenomenon has been called "de-standardization" and is something that can impact the assurance of corporate communications by provoking rapid migration from older telecoms services to new converged services.

De-standardization is the process by which regulated service providers are driving convergence through regulatory change requests.[17] Part of telecommunication regulation in most countries is that tariffs have to be filed for all services and the commencement and cession of telecoms services has to be approved. Service providers are actively seeking to re-define legacy services (old technologies with falling demand) with regulatory agencies in a process known as "de-standardization." Service providers seek de-standardization when a particular service technology is no longer profitable because demand may have disappeared or it has simply been superceded by

---

[16] The Anarchists Cookbook (Addendum): Start Your Own Telco!, Seaboard Group, May 2005.
[17] Bell Seeks Eased Service Withdrawal; Teleco Wants Speedier Destandardization, Perry Hoffman, Telemanagement, No. 222, Feb 2005.

better alternatives. As a result, the service provider makes a regulatory application to cease supporting that service under controlled tariffs because they would be losing money otherwise. De-standardization can mean two distinct things to convergence:

1. That service providers no longer must offer legacy telecom services (IE, switched, low-bandwidth, low yield services) at the same regulated tariff; thus, clients that wish to remain with legacy services can experience dramatic price increases once regulation is lifted (de-standarized).
2. Carriers no longer must offer the legacy service at all.

In either case, the customer who may have found legacy services to be perfectly adequate and have no reason to adopt new technology are being pressed into a migration. This migration is invariably toward converged IP solutions, because this is where the service providers are offering the alternative services to supplant legacy services.

Legacy services are often maintained as a matter of regulatory edict far past the point at which their margins have become unacceptable from a business perspective. Without regulation, a service provider would raise the price of a legacy service to maintain margins and force attrition in the service. In an environment where all services were available until the last subscriber disappears, business would move from the legacy services to newer cheaper services at their own pace, according to the relative financial burden of the transition versus benefits of the transition. With regulation, and the de-standardization process, businesses may experience a convergence whiplash as service providers abruptly increase the costs of legacy services or simply cancel services. At that point business are forced to make rapid decisions about the critical communications services that can impact the assurance of their organizational telecommunications significantly.

THE CONFLICTING PRIORITIES OF CONVERGENCE

Convergence should not be thought of as merely an efficient process of placing more applications and services on the same network; convergence must also be considered from the perspective of the aggregation of all the integration and communications assurance requirements in a single asset—the network. This translates to the convergence of not just the integration and communication data but the sensitivity of these data as well.

Complicating the nature of ICT security under convergence is the matter that different converged assets have different requirements related to the assurance "trinity" of confidentiality, integrity, and availability.

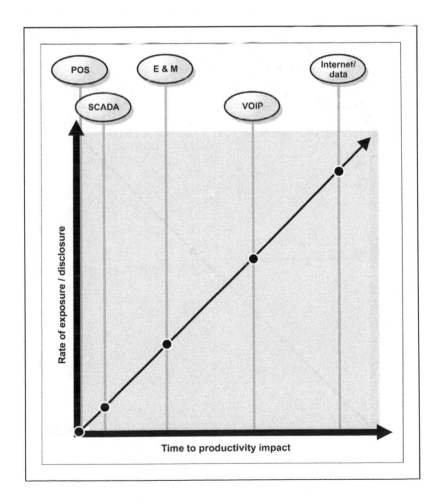

Chapter 2 of this book will seek to understand in greater detail how to measure the sensitivity and assurance requirements of different data assets. How much does your back-office data mean to your business? How much does your telephony system mean? How much might a remote-monitoring system matter? How much do they all mean together to be supported as a whole and possibly to disappear or be compromised as a whole? Different means of measuring sensitivity of individual assets will be suggested and a framework to better understand the converged sensitivity of these assets will be proposed, with the premise being to expose the resulting sensitivity

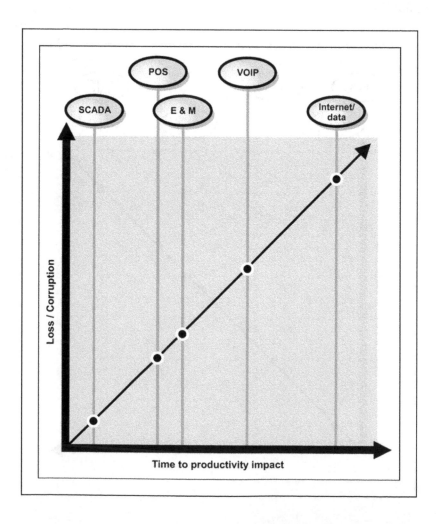

of converged assets, and show how they are greater than the sum of the parts.

In Chapter 3 of this book we will be discussing a wide range of ICT security threats and vulnerabilities that represent specific considerations for businesses commencing or in the midst of a transformation to a converged, all-IP world. These considerations spring from a single premise: that all of the applications converging onto IP currently have some degree of uniqueness in their legacies and therefore unique technical requirements and characteristics which may conflict. Business must understand this conflict of priorities and be prepared

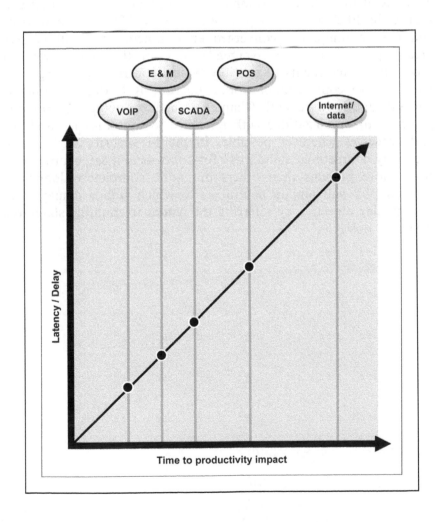

to carefully balance them in order to maintain the assurance of not just the IP network, but of all the converged applications now sharing the network. As for the converged applications we have called Blue Sky, these too will one day bring new requirements and new assurance priorities, but these requirements will be framed by the contemporary crop of converging applications. Blue Sky convergence is not a specific part of this discussion going forward for this reason.

After reviewing how an organization's ICT assets are impacted by convergence and the changes to threat and vulnerability profiles, we will consider ICT security counter-measures: controls and safeguards. Chapter 4 will discuss controls and safeguards in terms of management, technical, and operational tools that can reduce the likelihood of wide range of risks. Many of these risks will not be unique to converged environments but will possess greater potency under convergence, and for this reason we will focus on enhancements to possibly typical controls and safeguards particular to converged networks, but not ICT security controls and safeguards in general. Chapter 4 further attempts to provide guidance to organizations with reference to well-known standards and processes wherever possible. In the IT security world there are many competing "standards" for controls and safeguards, with some more popular than others but none completely dominant. This chapter will remain neutral as to which standard may meet a particular objective by referring the reader to multiple standards wherever possible.

Chapter 5 will provide recommendations for managing the assurance, implementation and operation of converged ICT network infrastructures. This chapter will continue discussion of qualitative and quantitative security metrics from Chapter 2, and the employment of metrics as a management tool. Again, there are a variety of different systems and "standards" available to measure security processes, the most popular of these will be summarized and discussed in Chapter 5. This chapter will conclude with some recommendations for the development and deployment of metrics systems under different convergence scenarios; for instance, a "mildly" converged environment with simply data and voice telephony on IP, versus a "intensely" converged environment with full Triple Play convergence plus several Transparently converged systems or applications.

Chapter 6, the final chapter, will look at the future of ICT security and assurance under IP convergence. What are the new tools and techniques that may arise to address or streamline the issues presented in this book? What is on the edge of or over the horizon as far as new management and technical techniques are concerned? In which directions will the new requirements generated by convergence and converged sensitivity drive organizations and businesses of all types and sizes?

Converged Sensitivity and Enterprise Risk Management

AUTHOR: Tyson Macaulay
Bell Security Solutions, Inc.

CONTRIBUTING AUTHOR: Phil Norton
A.J. Gallagher & Co.

INTRODUCTION

Converged sensitivity describes the impact of ICT convergence on the assurance requirements of information assets in an organization. Converged sensitivity is about comprehending that the risks and assurance requirements of available assets cannot be considered independently if an organization wishes to take advantage of converged IP applications. Enterprise risk managers have always said that assurance and risk must be gauged across the entire organization and must take into account all assets; this approach to risk management has taken on a significantly new meaning in the all-IP world. Converged applications penetrate all levels of production and lines of business and the segregated and redundant integration and communications systems of old are gone. Convergence presents a new potential for threats that impact across organizations and results in cascading failures not been previously known.

TARGET AUDIENCE

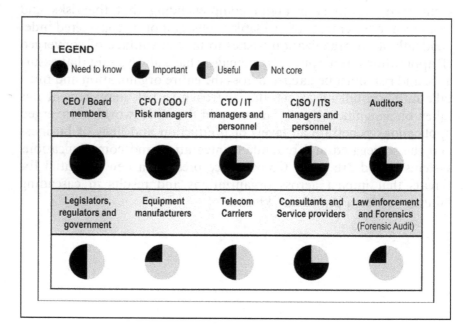

A WHOLE GREATER THAN THE SUM OF ITS PARTS

Converged sensitivity is the recognition that the combination of multiple information assets (data, voice, entertainment and media, industrial controls, physical security, etc.) on a common IP medium results in an amalgamated sensitivity that is substantially increased beyond the prosaic sum of the individual assets' sensitivities. Note that converged sensitivity runs counter to typical risk aggregation, as most business risks are correlated in a way that reduces their prosaic sum of the risk factors:

$\text{Sensitivity}_1 + \text{Sensitivity}_2 + \dots \text{Sensitivity}_N$
  $< \text{Highest sensitivity of any given asset}$

The opposite is true in the world of converged sensitivity:

$\text{Sensitivity}_1 + \text{Sensitivity}_2 + \dots \text{Sensitivity}_N$
  $> \text{Sensitivity of the most sensitive asset, as just noted.}$

Chapter 1 started by defining the sensitivity of a given information asset as the combined requirements (regulatory or otherwise) around *confidentiality, integrity*, and *availability*, with "assurance" being a level of confidence that these requirements are being fulfilled. A task of all stakeholders of an information asset is to maintain and ensure the assurance of all assets on converged networks. The central issue that organizations and enterprises must contend with in the all-IP world is that requirements around sensitivity must be viewed and calculated in a new way, taking into account not just assurance of the most sensitive asset but the impact on business and technical requirements of the converged sensitivity.

Typically, the sensitivity of an information asset—such as email—would be set according to the sensitivity and assurance requirements related to the *most* sensitive data managed within the asset. For instance, most email traffic on a enterprise network will be mundane if not banal—administrative matters or even chit-chat. However, some extremely sensitive corporate information such as financial projections, merger or acquisition data, or regulatory information will also be carried over this enterprise network and managed within the enterprise email servers. If this is the case, the overall sensitivity requirements and assurance of the network and email servers should meet the minimum requirements of the most sensitive data.

The theoretical ramification of this assessment is that all desktops, networks, and email servers should be managed to provide the necessary assurance related to the most sensitive email messages. But let's not get carried away. This happens only in the highest assurance military or research environments where national security or incredibly valuable trade secrets are at stake. In reality, enterprises have two simple alternatives to address the assurance requirements of their own email systems: encrypt the sensitive email messages (assuming the confidentiality is the defining component of email sensitivity in this example enterprise to logically separate it from the less sensitive data), or do nothing and accept the risks.

Many companies are looking to a third method of providing assurance in the financial sense of the word by considering a cost-effective method of identifying the most sensitive email messages (which will, by nature of the fix, be less than perfect) by combining

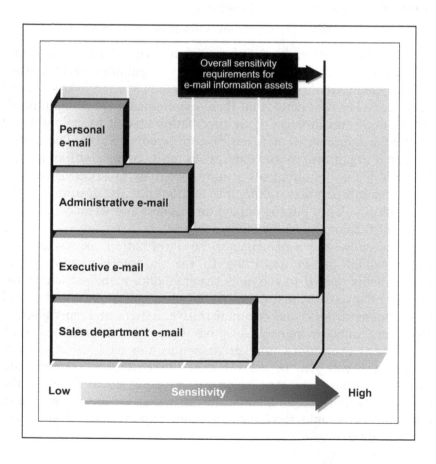

standard IT security safeguards with financial insurance in the event that: 1) the method fail to correctly identify and protect the sensitive email, and 2) the email is improperly distributed or otherwise compromised. For example, a pharmaceutical company employee emails confidential patient data to a series of wrong addresses. There is no method of identifying and catching the mistake and thus the message goes through. Insurance will then address the financial aspect of lawsuits that may follow as a result, yet it cannot adequately guard against damage to the company's "brand name." This example delivers home a critical point—the risk management aspect of dealing with converged sensitivity is often more important than the financial protections available through insurance.

Note also that maintaining extremely high levels of confidence regarding network assurance of sensitivity requirements could be prohibitively expensive. For example, consider the following table of potential cost factors:

Level of Information Asset Protection	Cost Factor
75th Percentile Confidence	1 X
90th Percentile Confidence	3 X
95th Percentile Confidence	6 X
99th Percentile Confidence	15 X
99.5[th] Percentile Confidence	30 X

For certain industries (perhaps banking, healthcare, energy, etc.), nothing less than a very high confidence level is acceptable. These industries have a program of ongoing network assessments (and remedies). Such evaluations and the subsequent improvements become crucial to the future success of their business. They also help protect themselves against the greater business volatility that results from IP convergence. How then do businesses reach an acceptable level confidence that they are adequately protected? It is the combination of enhanced network security (often through outsourcing to state-of-the-art business partners) plus financial insurance that will optimize company's overall network assurance on a dollar-invested basis.

Staying with the email example, most organizations just accept the risks and send all email over the same networks and through the same servers in the same manner. And for the most part, it works

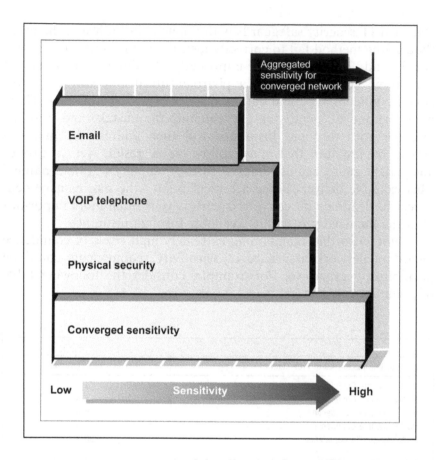

for many enterprises because the costs of supporting assurance for the most sensitive emails outweigh the cost of a compromise relative to the likelihood of the compromise occurring. It is simple math to them.

The math gets more difficult under ICT convergence. To start with, enterprises need to consider that the compromise of assurance in one converged information asset may lead to the compromise of assurance in the other converged assets. If your emails are being intercepted and read, then your VOIP telephone conversations are likely being intercepted as well. If the WAN drops and your VOIP phones are useless, it's possible that all your web-portal transactions with customers have also ceased. If they have not, certainly your ability to manage and monitor these transactions is significantly degraded, thereby degrading the assurance of the transactions themselves. These notions are relatively easy to understand in our email example—under ICT convergence, add the risks and costs together to get a sum of the total risks and costs, and assume that the assurance requirement for all assets is equal to the highest requirement among the group of assets. However, this is an inaccurate and incomplete picture of the impact of convergence on the assurance requirements of the enterprise IP network. The assurance requirement of the enterprise network reflects the converged sensitivity of all the information assets, and is actually greater than the requirement of the most sensitive, individual asset. Because the elements of an enterprise network are inter-related, to run your business better, they must also be more inter-dependant than ever. This business coordination, while positive and powerful, means greater risk and thus demands greater protection.

Understanding the phenomena of converged sensitivity is about two distinct pieces of information: one simple to grasp and one far more complex.

First, redundancy is not as simple as it once was. Many assumptions around redundancy may linger in organizations even as they converge their data assets. Whereas before we had independent networks for email and telephone and physical security, we now have one monolithic network. In "the old days" you could pick up a phone and call for information if email was non-functional. But today, if you can't email, phone or even print, and the door strikes are off-line and will not let you back into the office if you leave—you are essentially incapacitated. Calculations around the risks associated with a non-converged information asset assumed independent networks and infrastructure—and therefore redundancy—was a mitigating safeguard. As a result, those old risk calculations are no longer accurate. They over-estimate available safeguards and under-estimate both the impact and likelihood of threats. However, the impact of converged sensitivity is not completely additive. For example, while the converged sensitivity "sum" in the above bar chart is larger than the maximum of the sensitivities of the three information assets, it is also smaller than the sum of those three bars. This reflects the "portfolio view" of risk, described later in the section on enterprise risk management.

Second, the convergence of information assets has an enterprise-wide impact, from production capabilities to public address systems to 911 services. As a result, Enterprise Risk Management (ERM) techniques need to be applied to the understanding of converged sensitivity and the management of ICT convergence.

The next section will discuss the principles of Enterprise Risk Management and how managers can apply them to understand and deal with converged sensitivity.

ENTERPRISE RISK MANAGEMENT AND IP CONVERGENCE

Convergence is a practical problem that Enterprise Risk Management (ERM) frameworks were developed to solve. In this section we will explore the nature of ERM as it may be applied to convergence: What is ERM? What are some of the techniques employed in ERM? And how could an ERM program account for convergence issues such as converged sensitivity?

What Is ERM?

The most frequently cited work in the area of ERM is the Enterprise Risk Management—Integrated Framework from the Committee of Sponsoring Organizations of the Treadway Commission (COSO), which was published in September of 2004 after three years of effort. The impetus for the COSO ERM framework was essentially the bursting of the dot-com bubble and the financial scandals that resulted. The terrorist attacks of September 2001, however, added even more meaning and dimension to this project and the resulting tools.

ERM allows and supports an integrated organizational response to risk, from the setting of objectives for risk management to assessing risks to implementing and monitoring risks. An ERM process should look across the organization and provide insight into not only the risks facing an organization but also expose potential business opportunities associated with improving efficiencies and even the introduction of new products. For instance, ERM may reveal significant risks to an order-taking application, but at the same time engender an out-sourcing solution that saves money. Alternately, a review of the order-taking application process-flows may reveal that new product bundles would increase sale and tap new market, creating a new business opportunity. As COSO puts it:

> Enterprise risk management requires an entity to take a *portfolio view* of risk. This might involve each manager responsible for a business unit, function, process, or other activity developing an assessment of risk for the activity. The assessment may be quantitative or qualitative. With a composite view at each succeeding level of the organization, senior management is positioned to make a determination whether the entity's overall risk portfolio is commensurate with its risk appetite.

Management considers interrelated risks from an entity-level portfolio perspective. Risks for individual units of the entity may be within the units' risk tolerances, but taken together may exceed the risk appetite of the entity as a whole. Or, conversely, potential events may represent an otherwise unacceptable risk in one business unit, but with an offsetting effect in another. Interrelated risks need to be identified and acted on so that the entirety of risk is consistent with the entity's risk appetite.[1]

The notion of converged sensitivity is derived from this larger and well-established component of ERM known as "entity-level risk," which is the process of aggregating the sensitivity of all assets and the risks facing these assets to come out with a single, finite level of sensitivity and risk assessment.[2] The trick to arriving at entity-level estimations of risk and sensitivity is the ability to utilize systems of metrics that employ common scales and measures, so they can be aggregated. Alternately, if it is not obvious or is too complex to try and employ common scales and metrics, management can always make or sanction subjective decisions about the inter-relationships between the sensitivity of one converged asset and another. The issue of subjective decisions versus objective decisions leads to the key concept of metrics.

In all management domains there are fundamentally two types of metrics that may be employed to support management decisions: qualitative and quantitative. The differences are substantial and many managers will have been unconsciously trained to fear them both as complex and esoteric, with one actually being worse than the other! Before we consider the distinctions, let us consider one important point about the usage of metrics in the management of converged sensitivity—scope.

The scope of this discussion around ERM and metrics is the convergence of information and communication assets in the all IP world. This makes a big difference to the employability of the advice and techniques contained in this book because while we are still talking about distinct applications and services, we are always talking about

---

[1] Enterprise Risk Management—Integrated Framework: Framework, COSO, Sept 2004, pg 19.
[2] Enterprise Risk Management—Integrated Framework: Application techniques, COSO, Sept 2004, pg 52.

data and IP assets. Most ERM engagements would need to consider not just data but tangible widgets and all the supporting production inputs and processes. In our case there is one widget—"data"—and one major input—"IP" networks. Similarly, because all converged applications can be reduced to "data on IP" they are largely susceptible to the same threats and therefore have many common approaches to both qualitative and quantitative analysis.

Metrics: Qualitative and Quantitative

In this section we will consider the distinction between qualitative and quantitative metrics. For information about techniques specific to the collection of risk metrics around converged applications, please see Chapter 5: Managing Assurance.

> Management often uses qualitative assessment techniques where risks do not lend themselves to quantification or when either sufficient credible data required for quantitative assessments is not practically available or obtaining or analyzing data is not cost-effective. Quantitative techniques typically bring more precision and are used in more complex and sophisticated activities to supplement qualitative techniques.[3]

Qualitative Metrics

Qualitative techniques tend to be more subjective and supplied by people as opposed to metrics derived through mathematically analysis. Qualitative metrics take subjective terms such as "not important/ important" or "trivial impact/grave impact" and convert these subjective terms to numerical values. A typical example is a risk matrix which derives a risk metric from subjective qualitative inputs around the likelihood of a threat and the resulting potential impact. For example:

> *The Threat*: A worm or virus will penetrates the perimeter network defenses.

---

[3] Enterprise Risk Management - Integrated Framework: Application Techniques, COSO, Sept 2004, pg 35.

Likelihood Question: What is the likelihood that a worm or virus will penetrate the perimeter network defenses in the next 2 years and flood the network with traffic (the threat), resulting in an outage?
Answer: Likely

Impact Question 1: What would be the impact of losing back-office data access for 1 day?
Answer: Moderate

ALTERNATE QUESTION:
Impact Question 2: What would be the impact of losing VOIP telephony for 1 day?
Answer: Moderate

ALTERNATE QUESTION:
Impact Question 3: What would be the impact of losing both back-office data and VOIP telephony for 1 day?
Answer: Severe

Next, apply the comparative risk metrics from the table below.

Risk Matrix

Impact/Likelihood	Unlikely	Likely	Very Likely
Minimal	1	3	6
Moderate	2	5	8
Severe	4	7	9

As a result, the following comparative metrics around the different scenario questions result.

Risk Result Comparison

Impact 1	Impact 2	Impact 3
5	5	7

The quality of qualitative metrics depends very heavily upon the expertise, professionalism and potential bias of the people providing the judgments. For this reason qualitative metrics are subject to a substantial margin of error relative to their quantitative counterparts. "Quantitative assessment techniques usually require a higher degree of effort and rigor [than qualitative techniques], sometimes using mathematical models. Quantitative techniques are highly dependent on the quality of the supporting data and assumptions, and are most relevant for exposures that have a known history and frequency of variability and allow reliable forecasting."[4]

Quantitative Metrics

Quantitative measures are more complex to gather and requirement more effort to manage than qualitative measures, because they are often derived directly from events or logs that have units of measure associated with them. For instance, latency is measured in milliseconds (an interval metric) or perhaps packet-loss measures as a percentage (a ratio measurement).

However, there are challenges to the employment of quantitative metrics in the ERM world because of the fact that aggregation up to entity-level risk and sensitivity requires the combination of metrics from a wide variety of sources that may utilize entirely different measurement systems. As examples, the Human Resources (HR) department may use rates of personnel attrition and health claims as a measure of the sensitivity of the HR asset; the Finance department may use share value to measure the sensitivity of cost-of-capital; and Operations may use a productivity measurement for the sensitivity of capital assets. Trying to distill this information into a meaningful entity-level risk assessment eventually requires subjective judgments by management about how one form of quantitative measurement equates to another form of measurement, and in the end your quantitative metrics may end up as qualitative measures (Fig. 1).

The use of quantitative metrics is much less likely to revert to a qualitative measure if the application is the measurement of the converged sensitivity of IP assets. This holds true for the simple reason that the converged assets all have significant commonality

---

[4] Enterprise Risk Management—Integrated Framework: Framework, COSO, Sept 2004, pg 52.

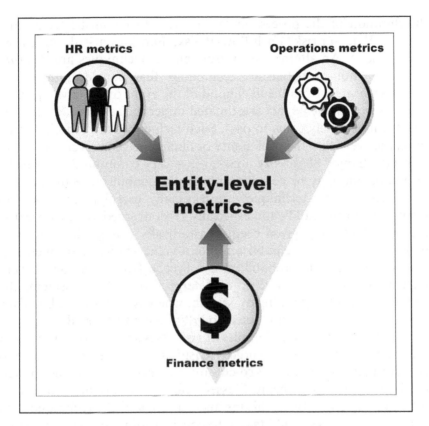

Figure 1: Quantitative metrics from different lines of business.

in that they use the same physical and logical network pathways and resources; there are many common measurements of sensitivity. The exact nature and variety of these measurements is the topic of Chapter 5: Managing Assurance. The remainder of this chapter will continue to discuss the nature of quantitative metrics and ERM.

Quantitative Techniques

One popular technique for the generation of quantitative techniques is known as the *probabilistic* technique, namely "projections that consider the probability of various events occurring to individuals over the duration of the process under study."[5] Probabilistic techniques include: Value-at-risk, Cash-flow-at-risk, Earnings-at-risk, and Loss distributions. An alternative to probabilistic techniques are *deterministic* or "non-probabilistic" techniques that consider impact of events separately from the likelihood of the event over a given period. In other words, the impact is estimated under the assumption that the event will definitely come to pass. Such techniques are especially useful in the event that the probability or likelihood of an event is subject to rapid change. Sensitivity analysis is a very common deterministic technique and may be complemented by probabilistic techniques.

Deterministic techniques are especially useful in the management of risk around IT- and especially IP-converged systems because the probability of a given event can radically change literally overnight. For instance, the publication of a vulnerability in an operating system can take the probability of a breach from very low to very high immediately. In the case of deterministic risk assessment, the impact on sensitivity is already known, whereas under a probabilistic risk assessment the calculations would all have to be re-done!

Yet, probabilistic techniques of risk assessment play a important role in understanding converged sensitivity because they take into account factors that are not so cut-and-dry, such as as the net potential impact on converged ICT assets of an announcement of a new software vulnerability. In this instance, a probabilistic technique such as cash-flow-at-risk would take into consideration not just the impact on assurance but also the *impact on cash flow and profits*.

> [Cash-flow-at-risk] estimates a change in the cash flows of an organization or business unit relative to a targeted cash flow expectation with a given confidence over a defined time horizon. This is based on distributional assumptions about the behavior of changes in cash flows. Cash flow at risk is used for businesses whose results are sensitive to changes in cash flows related to non-market-price factors.[6]

This is the crux of converged sensitivity: It must be considered and measured using a hybrid approach to risk assessment and

---

[5] http://www.google.ca/search?hl=en&lr=&oi=defmore&q=define:probabilistic.

[6] Enterprise Risk Management—Integrated Framework: Application Techniques, COSO, Sept 2004, pg 40.

management; combining qualitative and quantitative, deterministic and probabilistic techniques to tease out the scope of the entire impact of a potential ICT event on the organization/enterprise as a whole. Traditionally, ICT risks are assessed using deterministic, qualitative techniques (see NIST 800-55: Security Metrics Guide for Information Technology Systems[7] or the RCMP Guide to Threat Risk Assessment of Information Technology[8] for proof), but these will no longer suffice because they cannot accurately estimate the impact on an organization of assurance losses in converged ICT.

The remainder of this chapter will discuss the relationship and interface points between qualitative and quantitative metrics and how to effectively brew a ERM regime to both assess and manage the affects of converged sensitivity.

Selecting Risk Assessment Techniques for Converged Sensitivity

As we have seen, there are a wide range of techniques available for general risk assessment. These can be broken into a matrix defined by probabilistic and deterministic tools, and qualitative versus quantitative tools. The following table is a sample of the different risk assessment techniques available to managers.

Risk Assessment Tools Matrix

	Probabilistic Tools	Deterministic Tools
Quantitative Tools	• Statistical analysis • Value at risk • Cash flow at risk • Earnings at risk • Loss distributions • Back-testing	• Scenario planning • Sensitivity analysis • Stress testing • Benchmarking • Leading indicator analysis
Qualitative Tools		• Self-assessment • Business impact analysis • Qualitative prioritization • Risk indicator analysis

---

[7] http://csrc.nist.gov/publications/nistpubs/800-55/sp800-55.pdf.

[8] http://www.rcmp-grc.gc.ca/tsb/pubs/it_sec/g2-001_e.pdf.

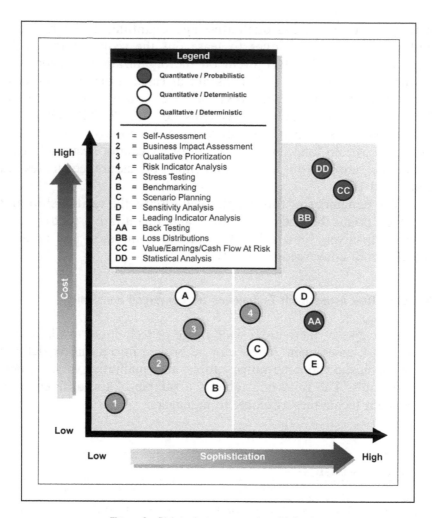

Figure 2 Risk tools by cost and sophistication.

The tools described in this table must also be understood from the perspective of the cost to implement and the degree of accuracy and sophistication they offer, with the cost to implement being a reflection of the difficulty of gathering and aggregating the necessary data and the time and skills required to do this in an accurate and valid fashion. Sophistication of a tool would refer to the ability of the tool to both accurately predict impact an event and, in the case of probabilistic tools, the likelihood of this event under different conditions.

Cost and sophistication are not the sole indicators of how risk tools should be selected, but they are frequently the most pertinent to organizations. Other important indicators of whether a tool is appropriate to organizations trying to assess the risks associated with converged sensitivity are:

- The severity or volatility of the risk
- The availability of metrics and data
- The desired capability to be derived from the tool

Increased severity or volatility of the risk(s) would generally dictate that more resources would be directed to managing the risks. Therefore the more expensive risk tools become viable in the context of a strong perception of risk. (Perception often being all that is really available in lieu of any formalized risk assessment). The availability of metrics and data to serve as inputs to the risk assessment tools is a primary concern and often represents a major cost-component in the development of tools. Sometimes the data have to be collected from multiple sources through lengthy processes, as in the case of most qualitative data that require interviewing and surveys. In other cases the data are readily available but so voluminous and dense with irrelevances (such as transaction log files) that the cleansing and processing of these data would require significant effort. Finally, what specifically is the expected information to be derived from the tool? Is a 5-year probability the objective or simply a 1-month probability? Vastly more research and data analysis are required in for the 5-year view compared to the 1-month view.

Seek Negative Correlations Among Risk Tools

One of the final points about the selection of risk management strategies around converged sensitivity is: Select tools that do not correlate. Correlation refers to the tendency of the same risk measurements to react in the same manner to the same event—in other words, they track each other or move synchronously. The obvious disadvantage of this is that, in the end, you might as well have used just one tool since the results will look nearly the same. Negative correlation is a basic tool of investors seeking to protect financial assets against major market moves. In the case of professional investors, they seek tools with low or negative correlation as a hedge, rather than as a validation tool as we are discussing. But the similarity of purpose is meaningful.

Low or negative correlation produces a portfolio diversification effect: the whole (combined risk) is less than the sum of its parts. How so? If multiple risk assessment tools (or even just two tools) are used with low or negatively correlated metrics, then the chances of false positives or false negatives are lower than in the case of reliance upon a single tool and metric. This is true simply because if both tools react to a potential threat, then the chances are greater that a real risk has developed. Low or negative correlation is essentially a hedge against what is known as *inherent risk*: the risk that your tools or processes do not perform as intended; i.e., they are not the valid risk assessment tools you thought they were. And the hedge works because of the reduced volatility that the portfolio approach brings about through such low or negative correlation.

Low or negative correlative between risk assessment tools is like receiving opinions from two completely independent, knowledgable doctors about a health condition and they both tell you the same thing. There is a good chance they are correct and you should act rather than merely consider the matter further. On the other hand, if you have a difference of opinion between two excellent, independent doctors, you assess a yellow flag on the condition and look more carefully into the matter immediately. The counterpart to this analogy is getting an opinion from two doctors in the same practice and they both give the same opinion; they may both be right, but they are also inclined to both be wrong at the same time because they possess a higher degree of correlation due to factors like proximity, familiarity, shared experiences, and backgrounds.

Diversify Tools by IP Asset

First, use more than one risk management tool. Second, seek low and negative correlation in risk tools. Third, the tools themselves should be based upon inputs that have been extracted from distinct, converged assets. This is a further possible technique to improve ERM under IP convergence. For instance, quantitative (or possibly qualitative) data from the VOIP and the back-office data systems feed into distinct risk tools with low or negative correlations. The advantage of this approach over just selecting any low or negative correlation tools is that the true nature of converged sensitivity is now being addressed: Threats that are invisible to one IP asset may be visible in another asset sooner—and sooner or later that threat will become visible to all IP assets because of the very nature of convergence.

Developing and implementing multiple, low or negative correlation risk assessment tools is a potentially costly exercise because these tools will need to be customized to each organization and infrastructure; however, there are significant advantages to employing ERM in this manner:

1. Low or negatively correlated risk tools, segregated by IP asset, balance and even counteract the affect of converged sensitivity resulting in a combined risk that is *less than the sum of its parts*.

2. Without considering negative correlation risks will be:
   a. Under or over estimated
   b. Mitigation will be under or over applied
   c. Risk transfers will be inefficient and costs will be out of line with risk reduction

These advantages amount to one of the core objectives of ERM: to both identify risks to an organization and identify opportunities. In this case the opportunity to deal with converged sensitivity of IP assets is such an effective matter that not only does a better, more secure ICT infrastructure result, but the costs associated with the assurance of the infrastructure decrease.

Portfolio Views of Risk Versus Converged ICT Assets

A portfolio view of risk is the generally advocated approach to ERM. As COSO puts it: "Enterprise risk management requires that risk be considered from an entity-wide, or portfolio, perspective. Management typically takes an approach in which risk first is considered for each business unit, department, or function, with the responsible manager developing a composite assessment of risks for the unit... [but] a portfolio view may be gained by focusing on major risks or event categories across business units."[9] This is the approach this book takes to ERM matters related to convergence: that

---

[9] Enterprise Risk Management - Integrated Framework: Framework, COSO, Sept 2004, pg 59.

converged sensitivity is a matter spanning not merely business units but business-risk categorizations.

While COSO makes the observation that establishing a portfolio view of risk according to business unit is "typical," an alternate view is by the type of business-risk event. This alternate view is a useful contrast to a business-unit view of risk for several reasons:

1. The focus is on how risk relates directly to losses, rather than how risk relates to business units which then impact other business units which, when combined, relate to losses. A risk event view goes straight to the point in some cases.
2. Two very distinct mitigating factors—Human Impact and Continuity (HI) and ICT—around business risks are considered as "horizontals" spanning all business risks and therefore the risks and related safeguards should span the organization.

Figure 3 summarizes the nature of an alternate view to ERM that focuses on business risk events rather than business units.[10] It is beyond the scope of this book to attempt to go into the detailed definition of the enumerated risks; however, more can be said about the mitigating verticals and how they relate to converged sensitivity and managing the assurance of converged IP networks.

HI is a topic also beyond the scope of this book but is so critical to ERM and the assurance of converged IP networks that it bares some mention. HI deals with the management and mitigation of risks associated with the loss, damage or interference with the people-components of a business or organization. How people react to different threats and risks and what the impact (amplification) will be on all the business-risks and even ICT. In the end, a risk management, disaster recovery or business continuity plan is useless if there is no one around willing to implement it because they are too concerned for their family.

ICT and the converged IP assets represent another risk-event horizontal in ERM that impacts not only all business risks, but also all business units. This is especially true in a converged IP infrastructure where all information and communication run over IP. In this case, the assurance of ICT has a significant capability to mitigate business risks by improving predictability of impacts, reducing outages and response times, and overall reducing the business risk.

---

[10] Mercer Management Consulting.

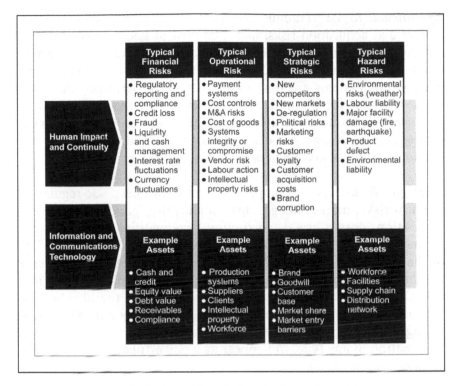

	Typical Financial Risks	Typical Operational Risk	Typical Strategic Risks	Typical Hazard Risks
Human Impact and Continuity	• Regulatory reporting and compliance • Credit loss • Fraud • Liquidity and cash management • Interest rate fluctuations • Currency fluctuations	• Payment systems • Cost controls • M&A risks • Cost of goods • Systems integrity or compromise • Vendor risk • Labour action • Intellectual property risks	• New competitors • New markets • De-regulation • Political risks • Marketing risks • Customer loyalty • Customer acquisition costs • Brand corruption	• Environmental risks (weather) • Labour liability • Major facility damage (fire, earthquake) • Product defect • Environmental liability
Information and Communications Technology	**Example Assets** • Cash and credit • Equity value • Debt value • Receivables • Compliance	**Example Assets** • Production systems • Suppliers • Clients • Intellectual property • Workforce	**Example Assets** • Brand • Goodwill • Customer base • Market share • Market entry barriers	**Example Assets** • Workforce • Facilities • Supply chain • Distribution network

Figure 3   Business-risk verticals and mitigating horizontals.

Let us consider examples from each of the business-risk verticals and determine how well managed converged sensitivity and network assurance can mitigate risks:

Financial Risks: Regulatory reporting and compliance, credit loss or down-grade, fraud, liquidity and cash management, interest rate fluctuations, currency fluctuations. Sarbanes Oxley (SoX) compliance is a large issue for many organizations today. Reporting requirements and the security and assurance of information management are core issues. A poorly managed converged ICT network with weak assurance introduces questions about the integrity of the reporting and impacts not only compliance, but threatens equity (market) values. Good assurance in both physical and converged IP infrastructure addresses compliance risks and could be seen as a market differentiator.

Operational Risks: Trading and payment systems, cost controls, merger and acquisition risks, increased cost of goods, command and control systems integrity or compromise, supplier risk, labor action, intellectual property risks. Both back-office systems and manufacturing controls systems are now running on ICT networks. A loss of one service could result in the loss of other inter-related assets, systems and services—both physical and logical—and result in production outages. Good assurance in converged IP infrastructure enhances production continuity and reduces overall operational risks.

Strategic Risks: New competitors, new markets, de-regulation, political risks, market image, customer loyalty, good will, customer acquisition costs, brand corruption, competitive processes and formulas. Loss of corporate Intellectual Property (the "other IP") or the perception of a weak competitive profile is partially addressable through demonstrably good assurance around physical and logical ICT infrastructures. Good assurance will limit the likelihood of the loss of IP related to technical failings (but only partially human failings!) and, especially in the services business related to personal information of any type, will appear as a powerful competitive differentiator and advantage.

Hazard Risks: Environmental risks (e.g., weather), labor liability, major facility damage (fire, earthquake), product defect liability, environmental liability. Acts of God and terrorism are possibly the most difficult threats to account for and provide safeguards against—whether they be physical safeguards or logical ICT safeguards. An organization must be able to demonstrate good physical and logical ICT assurance and safeguards around hazard risks, or should be able to substantiate their strategy around risk acceptance or transference.

CONCLUSION

This chapter introduced the notion of converged sensitivity: the sensitivity of the ICT network exceeds that of the most sensitive asset on that network. This is unlike typical ERM analysis, which sees aggregated sensitivity being lower than the sensitivity of the most sensitive asset on the network. The difference between typical ERM analysis and ERM under ICT convergence is that all assets are both physically and logically bound to a common (IP) network. What impacts one ICT asset will potentially impact the other assets; there is no subtlety about this relationship.

Management of ICT networks will be greatly improved and facilitated by the employment of metrics. This is a widely accepted risk management tenet at this point which must be applied to ICT assurance. Metrics endow an organization with the ability to track and compare safeguards and controls both between assets and over time, allowing for managed improvements and effective reporting to management concerning vital issues such as regulatory compliance and enterprise resiliancy. The question has now become: what sort of metric to employ? The proposed answer is that qualitative metrics are the current status quo and represent the lowest common denominator for most organizations. They are easiest to grasp and employ, and there are a variety of well-defined tools and methodologies to support implementation. Expensive expert-systems or consultants are not necessary. However, when it comes to metrics you get what you pay for: Qualitative metrics are course-grained (not very accurate or detailed) and will not remain the status quo for long. The risks facing converged ICT assets will, especially in large organizations, place pressure on management for more accurate and valid quantitative metrics. In fact, it is possible that in the future the use of quantitative metrics will become a matter of due-care from a regulatory perspective and the qualitative metrics that people are so impressed with today may actually become a form of negligence if they are the sole type of metric employed in the management of converged sensitivity.

A very useful counterpoint to the use of metrics in ERM and ICT networks is the use of insurance to transfer risk as opposed to constantly trying to employ further controls and safeguards. Insurance and risk management techniques go hand in hand. Insurance companies can leverage the metrics systems developed by organizations to price the cost of insurance in place of safeguards. Because an insurance company can aggregate the ICT risks across a wide range of clients, they can offer a more cost-effective solution to managing some share of most organizations ICT convergence risks.

The question is: What is this balance? The answer is related to what types of assets have been converged and what is the nature of the organization.

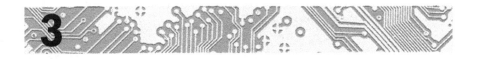

3

Information and Communications Technology (ICT) Threats and Vulnerabilities in the All-IP World

AUTHOR: **Tyson Macaulay**
Bell Security Solutions, Inc.

CONTRIBUTING AUTHORS: **Pritpal Bhogal**
Consultant
Robert Prudhomme
InCode Wireless

INTRODUCTION

This chapter will explore the emerging, real-world issues and threats facing the assurance of converged IP networks, and especially the assets which utilize these networks, whether they be the Triple Play or Transparent applications discussed in Chapter 1. These will be organized according to the type of convergence to which they are applicable, and we will attempt to highlight the distinction between a stand-alone impact on an asset and the impact on multiple converged assets; in other words, how a single type of threat presents risk to different converged assets.

Estimates on the likelihood of a given threat will be noted for the purposes of deriving qualitative risk calculations. Only significant threats will be enumerated in this chapter in order to manage its scope.

Furthermore, this chapter will focus on threats to assets and applications converging onto IP—the Triple Play (data, voice, and entertainment and media), Transparent convergence (physical security, facilities management, SCADA, financial transaction, and metering)—not "native" Internet threats. That is to say, specific, typical Internet-based threats such as Distributed Denial of Service (DDoS) attacks against web services will not be considered.

The following threats are discussed in this chapter:

Control Category	Threat Category
Management	• Walled gardens • Suppliers and contract management • Regulatory, archival, and lawful access requirements
Operational	• Location-implied functionality • Quality of service • Perimeter stress
Technical	• Electrical environment sensitivity • Soft devices • Green protocols, stacks, and architectures • End point security

TARGET AUDIENCE

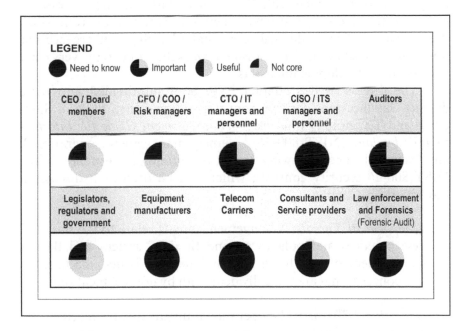

DESCRIPTIVE TECHNIQUES: RISK WORKSHEETS

In order to gain an understanding of the risks facing converged assets, they will be described using a standardized tabular format which draws heavily from traditional, formalized Threat Risk Assessment (TRA) processes and worksheets using qualitative metrics. In addition to the traditional descriptive techniques, we will also add a new dimension by simultaneously assessing a threat against multiple converged assets that may have different vulnerabilities and therefore different risks assessments. The purpose is to highlight the affects of converged sensitivity; impacts associated with ICT vulnerabilities are not necessarily limited to the assets against which they were targeted, or from which they originate. The reader will note that Blue Sky convergence has not been included in the risk assessment worksheet due to the very early state of these developmental assets.

The threats in this chapter have been sub-divided into three distinct classifications derived from the National Institutive of Standards and Technology's *Security Self-Assessment Guide for Information Technology* (NIST 800-26);[1] namely management, operational, and technical. The following threat-definitions correspond to the NIST 800-26 security controls, which will be used as a discussion framework in Chapter 4.

> *Management Threats*: Management threats relate to the business practices and policies around the ICT system and the management of risk for a system. They are issues, matters, and concerns that are typically dealt with by nontechnical staff.

> *Operational Threats*: The operational threats involve mechanisms primarily implemented and executed by people (as opposed to systems). These threats may impact individual systems, applications, and processes, or entire groups of systems, applications, and processes. They often derive from a lack of the required technical expertise or as a result of management lapses.

---

[1] NIST 800-26 - http://csrc.nist.gov/publications/nistpubs/800-26/sp800-26.pdf.

Technical Threat: Technical threats involve the potential for logical (through the network) and/or automated exploitation of ICT assets through software, protocols, or operating system flaws or misconfigurations. These threats may derive from malicious or benign entities and activities.

The organization of threats into management, operational, and technical is not typical of traditional threat-risk assessment processes. Threats are commonly classified according to the agent or event perpetrating the threat, or the type of threat relative to confidentiality, availability or integrity (which we collectively refer to as "assurance"). Traditional organization of threats is appropriate when assessing a relatively granular application, system, or process; however, when considering and organizing multi-dimensional, asset-level threats and risks, the use of the NIST classification scheme is more manageable and in fact intended for this purpose.

USE OF QUALITATIVE METRICS

The previous chapter had compared and contrasted qualitative metrics with quantitative metrics and put forward the opinion that quantitative metrics were more sophisticated and should be used as much as possible given resource constraints. However, in this section we are resorting to qualitative metrics in the risk worksheets being developed. Why?

Because these are purely example threats built around hypothetical organizations. There are not logs, events, dollars or widgets to count in order to provide quantitative assessments of these threats for the purposes of describing them to all readers. Additionally, as mentioned in Chapter 2, at the highest levels of the organization, management is often in the position of making subjective assessments about how different quantitative metrics relate to each other in order to arrive at a single, entity-level risk. Therefore, the use of qualitative metrics in this section is in part appropriate to the topic of considering asset-level risks associated with loss of assurance of the converged IP network.

Risk Matrix

Impact/Likelihood	Unlikely	Likely	Very Likely
Minimal	1	3	6
Moderate	2	5	8
Severe	4	7	9

THREAT LISTS

One final consideration around the exercise to follow against assets is that we are not attempting to present all known threats. The list of threats presented here has been specifically selected and developed to reflect newly developed, emerging, or largely unrecognized threats to converged assets. If the material from this book should be utilized in the course of developing threat assessments against converged assets, these threats and risks should be considered adjuncts to much larger, established and "known" threat lists that may contain hundreds of different items.

SAMPLE WORKSHEET

(See the following page for the Sample Worksheet)

Asset	Agent/Event	Class or Threat	Likelihood	Consequences of Occurrence	Impact	Exposure Rating	Existing Safeguards	Vulnerabilities	Risk
The specific type of converged asset	Describe the threat agent or event	Identify the class as: Confidentiality Availability Integrity	Assess the likelihood as: Low Medium High	Describe the consequence relative to the assets	Assess the injury as: Moderate Serious Grave	See Qualitative Exposure table from Chapter 2	What is done to counter this threat now?	How might a threat agent get past the safeguards?	Assess the risk as: Low Medium High
Data									
VOIP									
Entertainment and Media									
Physical									
SCADA									
Banking									
Facilities									
Metering									

Assessment Paradigm

The "reasonableness" of the assessment of a risk associated with a vulnerability is a subjective judgment based upon assurance requirements of a given asset and evidence of the existing safeguards. The assessments provided here are merely intended to be samples drawn against a hypothetical, large, converged organization with requirements for a commercial-grade of assurance for its assets. For our purposes, the definition of a commercial grade of assurance is one required to support entity-level risks (as discussed in Chapter 2: Financial Risks, Operational Risks, Strategic Risks and Hazard Risks) not for national-security purposes. Therefore, the assessment guidance provided in this chapter is not intended to support the entire range of assurance requirements possible. In some cases, too much assurance may be generated (assurance out of proportion to costs/ risks), and in other cases it is possible that too little assurance will be generated. Similarly, the safeguards that are assumed to exist reflect typical, known default configurations, architectures or security feature-sets associated with the given asset's hardware, software, and network characteristics. Organizations and readers will need to conduct their own internal sensitivity analyses in order to generate proper metrics and assessments around the value of their converged assets and thereby have a foundation upon which to judge the value of these sample assessments of threats and vulnerabilities.

MANAGEMENT THREATS

Management threats are threats related to the coordination of policies and practices concerning the ICT system and the management of risk. They are issues, matters and concerns that are typically dealt with at the senior levels of the organization.

Walled Gardens

"Walled Gardens" is a term that has been used to describe a variety of different product and market scenarios, but fundamentally refers to a vertically integrated supply and delivery environment where the customer experience is contained to a single brand that owns the "garden" in which the converged assets will function. Walled gardens are a management threat to organizations attempting to deploy and gain competitive advantage from converged assets because walled gardens reduce return-on-investment and foster supplier dependence.

To explain: any large organization, particularly those with extended, international presences, would like to be able to adopt converged technologies across the organization, not just within a campus or even a country. VOIP is an obvious example, because the ability to engage directly in inter-organizational, IP-based communication beyond data would also become a cost-saving boon. However, the status quo for employing converged applications is limited to the internal corporate LAN or, at best, the corporate WAN (the Walled Garden). Beyond that point, calls are dumped onto the legacy PSTN (Public Switched Telephone Network) for delivery. The reason for this is that the ISPs who supply bulk, broadband IP do not have peering or routing arrangements that take into account the requirements of clients outside there own networks. Information that must travel from one ISP to another is usually not routed in the most efficient manner, and the routes are not engineered to preserve the types of Quality of Service (QoS) that many converged applications require.[2] As a result, deployments of converged applications cannot be deployed across ISPs with the degree of assurance required for most businesses.

---

[2] David Clarke, Senior Research Scientist, MIT, presentation in New York City, July 21, 2005.

Most VOIP solution become a point solution instead of being enterprise solutions with the ability to support global integration.

Another contributing factor to the Walled Garden issue is the want of any reliable way of mapping phone numbers to IP addresses the way the existing, centralized and coordinated SS7 (PSTN) network does for switched phone calls. There are proposed solutions to mapping phones number to IP address (know as ENUM), whereby a VOIP proxy will call a mapping server that utilizes DNS (Domain Name Service) to do look-ups and determine routes. Unfortunately, DNS was never designed for security and a wide variety of attacks and vulnerabilities are associated with both the service and the protocol. ENUM may solve a management/ business threat with a technical threat of greater magnitude.[3] [ENUM RFC 3761 is a protocol the uses the Internet DNS system to translate E.164[4] (i.e., ordinary) telephone numbers into IP addressing schemes (like SIP, H323, or Email). RFC 3761 replaced the former RFC 2916 in May 2004.]

The delivery of Entertainment and Media and Digital Rights Management (DMR) through converged ICT networks is another form of Walled Garden. While there are ISO standards around DMR (for instance, ISO 21000[5]), there are no industry standards, the difference being that an industry standard has consumer forces behind it and manufacturers are compelled by the market to support particular technical capabilities. An ISO standard is merely a technical specification that has been agreed to by a group of industry peers. Entertainment and Media is the third part of the convergence Triple Play and includes products such as IPTV (television over IP networks), audio/video-on-demand, pay-per-view, and many other products. The DMR technologies that underpin the business model of Entertainment and Media convergence are currently very different from vendor to vendor, and even from network to network. For instance, Mpeg-21 (AKA Mpeg Rights Extension

---

[3] Baruch Sterman, VOIP value points must be addressed, Telemanagement No. 227, July-Aug 2005.

[4] http://www.voip-info.org/tiki-index.php?page=E.164.

[5] http://www.iso.ch/iso/en/CatalogueDetailPage.CatalogueDetail?CSNUMBER=35366& ICS1=35.

Language-REL) is supported by some of the largest vendors of fixed-line (set top/PC) devices such as Microsoft and RealNetworks. Yet mobile device manufacturers such as Samsung and Motorola are developing entirely different DMR technologies for their devices. Further to this point and similar to VOIP, DMR technologies will be entirely linked to the service provider who controls the Authorization, Access, and Accounting (triple-A) systems which facilitate the exchange of money for digital content. Once the device leaves the service provider environment, the chances that it will work with another service provider are slim.

This situation is a function of the early stages of DMR technologies and will be resolved–if service providers allow them to be resolved. Walled Gardens also exist for purely competitive reasons as well: they bind customers to service providers and force them to buy from a single storefront. DMR is yet another means for the service provider to generate more revenues from subscribers within their Walled Gardens, but to the potential disadvantage of the producers of content (artists) and the service provider themselves! For producers of the content that DMR technologies are supposed to benefit, Walled Gardens are simply the latest form of the older film and record/CD distribution and marketing cartels that used to control content, before Internet file-sharing brought them to their knees. DMR is controlled by the service providers in their Walled Gardens and if an artist wants to be in the Garden they have to abide by the service provider conditions and pay service provider royalties, which is further temptation for service providers to pursue Walled Gardens. Because the DMR and the triple-A infrastructure required to generate revenues require such a substantial investment and user-base, it is not very feasible to try and go independent *and* depend on DMR revenues for survival.

Walled Gardens around Entertainment and Media resulting from DMR imperil service providers because:

- The service provider is playing an all-or-none game. It risks losing customers because they want a particular, vogue product that is not available in the garden but a competitor has it on offer. The result is losing the customer entirely and increasing account "churn," coupled with unstable and pernicious cycles of feast and famine during and after "hits." This danger is compounded by the fact that most large ICT service providers will be selling multiple products to a majority of their customers; if the customer drops one product they are likely to drop the other products too, making for a multiple loss for the service provider.

- Walled Gardens are expensive to develop because they must be elaborate and fresh to keep people returning to the "same place" over and over. This investment increases the stakes for service providers of the all-or-nothing game.

Any decision to invest in converged assets should assume Walled Gardens and implement controls and safeguards to compensate.

Walled Gardens

Asset	Threat Assessment						Risk Assessment		
	Agent/Event	Class of Threat	Likelihood	Consequences of Occurrence	Impact	Exposure Rating	Existing Safeguards	Vulnerabilities	Risk
Data	• ISPs	Availability	High	Latency	Moderate	7	Natural environment for data, Native TCP/IP error correction and default routing	Lost ROI/productivity	Low
VOIP	• Routing practices • PSTN dependency	Availability	High	Reduced competitiveness and returns	Serious	8	Native TCP/IP error correction and default routing	Lost ROI, inability to scale investments	High
Entertainment and Media		Availability	High	Reduced selection	Grave	9	Isolated networks and proprietary devices	Lost customers/ROI	High
Physical	• DMR technology	Availability	High	Latency	Moderate	7	Native TCP/IP error correction and default routing, localized service requirements	Lost ROI, inability to scale investments	Low

(Continued)

Walled Gardens (*Continued*)

Asset	Threat Assessment						Risk Assessment		
	Agent/Event	Class of Threat	Likelihood	Consequences of Occurrence	Impact	Exposure Rating	Existing Safeguards	Vulnerabilities	Risk
SCADA		Availability	High	Latency	Moderate	7	Localized management, native TCP/IP error correction and default routing, localized service requirements	Lost ROI, inability to scale investments	Low
Banking		Availability	High	Latency	Moderate	7	Dedicated links, native TCP/IP error correction and default routing	Less ability to scale deployments rapidly	Low
Facilities		Availability	High	Latency	Moderate	7	Localized management, native TCP/IP error correction and default routing	Lost ROI, inability to scale investments	Low
Metering		Availability	High	Latency	Moderate	7	Native TCP/IP error correction and default routing, localized service requirements	Lost ROI, inability to scale investments	Low

Suppliers and Contract Management

The sensitivity and assurance requirements of the organizational IP network increases as more and more ICT assets converge upon it. As a result, the diligence associated with all elements of the network care-and-feeding increase. The stakes associated with ICT suppliers and contract management require executive level attention because of the potential impact of bad choices. It is often the case that supplier or vendor selection is left to relatively junior managers who make recommendations to senior managers. This system itself is not necessarily inappropriate, but senior management needs to establish the requirements for selection in an affirmative and detailed fashion and provide guidance around which particular conditions (threats) are to be observed and estimated.

Third-party services related to IP networks can take many forms: ISP services, network management services, equipment and hardware support, management software, and outsourced telephony (IP PBX) to name just a few potential options available to organizations. Each supplier will have a significant impact on the assurance of critical organizational assets: more so than in the past due to the convergence of these assets onto a single IP network. A new standard of diligence is required around the selection of these suppliers and the contracts that govern these relationships. While none of the material related to these contract management threats is new, the impacts on assurance when applied to converged networks has reached a never-before-seen criticality. This information is presented to enforce what is already considered management best practice around supplier and contract management, but has a new urgency under convergence.

Consider the stability of equipment providers. Will they be around to continue to service and support and especially patch the hardware/software that you have procured to manage the converged network? Software and protocol vulnerabilities are significant threats to converged networks and are constantly appearing in new forms:

The ability to have access to timely patches and fixes to hardware/ software components from reliable equipment providers is mandatory. A supplier that does not react in a timely way to vulnerabilities in its products (or has gone out of business or discontinued a product line) places the assurance of all converged assets at risk. Equipment providers that have the willingness and horsepower to contribute to standards development in forums like the International Standards Organization (ISO) are more likely to be in touch with evolving security issues and market trends. This translates into better awareness around the requirements for assurance of products.

Consider the stability of service providers such as ISPs or outsourced telephony services; for instance, managed IP PBX (VOIP) services. IP convergence potentially allows for the costs to be driven down by the emergence of outsourcing options for services that would previously have been available only from a narrow range of telecom providers. The result is a leveled playing field brought about by ICT convergence. But, sometimes a deal can be too good. Case in point: In March 2003, Level 3 Communications ceased to offer wholesale VOIP PBX to as many as 100 retail VOIP service providers, impacting thousands of end users and businesses in one stroke.[6] The profit margins in this business were not up to expectations and Level 3 quit the business. Suddenly, these retail service providers had to look for alternatives for all their clients and the assurance associated with crucial business telephony services evaporated. Part of the industry problem around outsourcing of ICT services to small players is that a typical business customer is 40 to 60 desks, which makes support costs high and economies of scale difficult to achieve. This further supports the requirement for caution when outsourcing converged ICT assets such as VOIP.

When outsourcing ICT assets or asset components, managers need to consider that two completely distinct organizations that will have access to the internal ICT traffic and the security control of the system as a whole will be no better than the worst controls within the weaker of the two entities.[7] In other words, you are not just outsourcing VOIP, you are outsourcing the assurance of a critical business asset. Does the service-provider have good logical security? Does the service provider have good security management practices, such as

---

[6] Reselling Hosted VOIP may not be as easy as it looks, Phone+, March 2005.
[7] The Value of VOIP Security, Mark Collier, SecureLogix, June 2004.

adherence to ISO 17799 or audits against service-provider assurance criteria such as CICA 5900 or SAS 70? Does the service provider screen its personnel and control access to infrastructure on a need-to-know basis, and segregate access using roles and logical controls?

Be cautious about great deals from third-party service providers. Be aware of certain expenses and costs that may not be included in the service and could wipe out savings. For instance, an outsourced IP PBX may require a significantly larger IP pipe with associated costs. If the provider of the service is not an ISP, they will probably have little visibility into the service contract currently in place and can only offer general market advice about where a good deal might be had and how to negotiate it. But that does not take into account the significant hassle and costs associated with switching ISPs. The philosophy in the converged ICT network with multiple assets on IP (XoIP) is to have a single logical network pipe into the premises and provide all services in that single pipe (i.e., the Triple play—Voice, Entertainment, and Data). Manufacturers must be aware that this model brings the complexity of managing a high-bandwidth pipe and demands more complex internal switching capabilities. This, in turn, can introduce more management and services costs, which are not very transparent initially when the implementation is planned. Under-provisioning is one of the main concerns of dealing with boutique service-providers.

A further reason to be cautious with smaller suppliers of IP-based services is that in the future they may as well be Russian dolls as far as the end-user is concerned: you really don't know who you are dealing with. Consider British Telecom, which has been compelled by regulators to provide equal access to wholesale bandwidth from its core national network to third parties. These third parties then sell to localized retailers, who then sell onto end users (organizations/consumers).[8] The result is that there are as many as two layers of supplier between the owner of the core network (probably the incumbant Tier 1 teleco) and the end-user. Wholesalers of bandwidth by necessity will sell to multiple retailers of bandwidth. These relationships will not be transparent to the end users. Therefore, the failure of single or multiple wholesalers could impact dozens of retailers and thousands of end-user organizations and tens of thousands of

---

[8] Daryl Dunbar, British Telecom, New York presentation, July 21, 2005.

users. If an organization has taken the sage and relatively common precaution of buying redundant bandwidth, they may find out the hard way that the redundancy they had purchased through distinct retailers was moot, since they both used the same wholesaler!

Possibly the most important consideration in supplier and contract management has to do with Service-Level Agreements (SLAs). SLAs govern the relationship between the external network provider/ISP and the organization. Key metrics contained within SLAs may be availability and uptime, throughput speed, error rate, packet lost rate, and possibly the number of network hops to major network peers. The higher the requirements around metrics such as availability and throughput/speed, the more expensive the SLA and resulting network contract will be because the costs of provisioning these sorts of services can increase substantially, especially once you start getting into "high availability." Most internet SLAs available "off the shelf" today were written for Internet data applications only and are poorly suited to support real-time applications in the Triple Play style of convergence. Similarly, these same SLAs will not support the determinism of Transparent convergence where sensitivity to error rates and data loss require high performance.

Supplier and Contract Management

Asset	Agent/Event	Class of Threat	Likelihood	Consequences of Occurrence	Impact	Exposure Rating	Existing Safeguards	Vulnerabilities	Risk
			Threat Assessment					Risk Assessment	
Data	• Stability of suppliers/ service providers	Confidentiality Availability	High	Loss of service, unauthorized access to communications	Grave	9	Typically ad hoc	Lost ROI, lost production, lost competitiveness	High
VOIP	• Weaker security posture of third-party providers	Confidentiality Availability	High	Loss of service, unauthorized access to communications	Grave	9	Typically ad hoc	Lost ROI, lost production, lost competitiveness	High
Entertainment and Media	• Hidden costs of outsourcing	Availability	High	Loss of service	Serious	8	Typically ad hoc	Lost ROI, lost production, lost competitiveness	High
Physical	• Providers as unaccountable Russian dolls	Availability	High	Loss of service	Serious	8	Localized management	Lost ROI, inability to scale investments	High
SCADA	• SLA conditions	Confidentiality Availability	High	Loss of service, unauthorized access to communications	Grave	9	Localized management	Lost ROI, lost production, lost competitiveness, lost workplace health and safety	High

(Continued)

Supplier and Contract Management (Continued)

| Asset | Agent/Event | Threat Assessment | | | | | | Risk Assessment | | |
		Class of Threat	Likelihood	Consequences of Occurrence	Impact	Exposure Rating	Existing Safeguards	Vulnerabilities	Risk
Banking		Confidentiality, availability	High	Loss of service, unauthorized access to communications	Moderate	7	Dedicated links	Lost ROI, lost production, lost competitiveness	Low
Facilities		Confidentiality, availability	High	Loss of service, unauthorized access to communications	Serious	8	Localized management	Lost ROI, lost production, lost competitiveness, lost workplace health and safety	Medium
Metering		Confidentiality, Availability	High	Loss of service, unauthorized access to communications	Serious	8	Native TCP/IP error correction and default routing	Lost ROI, lost revenue, lost competitiveness	High

Regulatory, Archival, and Lawful Access Requirements

Regulatory requirements around the preservation of personal privacy, financial reporting, and the maintenance of business records require careful evaluation of the corporate capabilities for maintaining electronic communications records and the assurance of converged assets.

On the next page is a sample list of the regulatory statutes that generate legal requirements around data and records management impacting converged communications applications.

While many managers may not fully understand the current regulatory implications of normal IP data applications, fewer still have an inkling of the implications of regulatory requirements as multiple ICT assets converge on IP. This is not to say that people are entirely uneducated in these matters; it is a case of the regulatory implications being often vague and unproven. Uncertainty around the intent of legislation vis-à-vis converged ICT assets increases the risk of regulatory breach.

Consider a logical extension of regulatory requirements around data retention requirements; VOIP voice mail archiving may be covered because these messages are in fact just data files like email. Few people may be considering the issues around the management of voice mail messages under convergence. VOIP voice mail has many challenges that go beyond regular email archiving:

- Larger audio files
- Very difficult to search for content in the event of a warrant (listen to each one?)
- Temporal challenges—an email is generally moved to a "deleted" folder well before it is really deleted. Therefore is can be backed up on a nightly incremental basis. Voice mails are usually deleted permanently once the person hangs-up from the voice-mail manager; messages may only have a lifetime measured in minutes. How do you preserve them? Do vendors support "deleted" folders right now?

Act	Retention Requirements
Sarbanes Oxley[9]	• 5 Year maintenance • Brokers/dealers to retain communications documents whether paper or electronic, including email and instant messages . . . to start
SB1386 in California[10]	• Immediate ability to reproduce documents • Data must be securely managed • Requirement for notification of potential compromise
Securities and Exchange Commission Rules 17a-3 and 17a-4[11]	• Easy availability of records • Retention from 2 to 6 years
Gramm–Leach–Bliley[12] (Financial Modernization Act of 1999)	• Data must be securely managed • Negative requirement—personal information should not be re-disclosed without permission and should not be retained without the ability to opt-out of retention
PIPEDA (Canada)[13]	• Data must be securely managed • Negative requirement—personal information may only be retained as long as required to satisfy the purpose for which is was required, then must be destroyed
EU Data Protection Act[14]	• Proposed 1 to 2-year data retention of telephony and ISP traffic for security purposes[15] • Negative requirement—personal information may only be retained as long as required to satisfy the purpose for which is was required, then must be destroyed

Uniform Electronic Transactions Act (UETA) of 1999[16]

HIPPA[17]
US Patriot Act[18]
UK Anti-Terrorism, Crime and Security Act[19]
Basel II[20]

- Model law for states
- Requires retention of records
- Requires accuracy and security in retention of records
- Maintain medical records for 5 to 10 years
- Section 815 maintain audit trails
- 12 Month retention of data traffic
- Banks retain 2 to 10 years of historical transaction data

[9]http://news.findlaw.com/hdocs/does/gwbush/sarbanesoxley072302.pdf.
[10]http://info.sen.ca.gov/pub/01.02/bill/sen/sb_1351-1400/sb_1386_bill_20020830_ebrolled.pdf.
[11]http://www.sec.gov.
[12]http://www.ftc.gov/privacy/glbact/glbsub1.htm.
[13]http://www.privcom.gc.ca/legislation/02_06_01_e.asp.
[14]http://www.dataprotection.ie/documents/legal/CompendiumAct.pdt.
[15]http://www.theregister.co.uk/2002/08/28/eu_to_force_isps.
[16]http://www.law.upenn.edu/bll/ulc/fnact99/1990s/ueta99.htm.
[17]Health Insurance Portability and Accountability Act.
[18]http://frwebgate.access.gpo.gov/cgi-bin/getdoc.cgi?dbname=107_cong_public_laws&docid=f:pub1056.107.pdf.
[19]UK Anti-Terrorism, Crime and Security Act, Part 11 Retention of Communications data.
[20]http://www.bis.org/publ/bcbs107.pdf.

Retention issues may also extend to CCTV records, which are digitally archived using DVR-type technologies and will clearly contain information that can confirm or deny the interaction of people at given places and times. This is potentially important information in the event of criminal investigations. While these examples of Transparent convergence share the same IP network, they may not be easily integrated into the same archive processes as data and voice, leading to more regulatory challenges around ease of availability:

- How do you search video archives for content?
- How many different archive processes are we going to require?

Privacy

The privacy implications of personal information sent and received as Internet data are well known and documented and will not be reviewed here. We are concerned primarily with the privacy implications of the assets converging on IP.

Legislation and regulatory requirements around the protection of personal information and privacy is now nearly universal in the OECD countries. These laws existing at a variety of levels of government—often overlapping with each other—and are frequently founded upon an original set of ten privacy principles that originated within the OECD in 1980.[21] It is not within the scope of this book to discuss the specific nature or compare and contrast the large body of distinct legislation around privacy; however, it is of value to review the seminal OECD principles because they provide significant insight into the form and affect of much privacy legislation around the world.

Privacy legislation will typically deal with the following issues: placing limits on the collection of personal information to minimal requirements; purpose of collection should be stated up front; personal information should not be used for any other purpose than that for which is was collected; personal information must be protected; management practices and policies concerning personal information should be transparent to the subject; individuals have the right to

---

[21] http://www.occd.org/document/18/0,2340,en_2649_34255_1815186_1_1_1_1,00. html.

know what information is held and correct mistakes, and holders of personal data should be accountable.

The convergence of formerly stove-piped communications systems offers a potential bonanza of knowledge about individuals via the central networks devices through which much of these data must pass. Firewalls and other devices will be logging converged information, which could have serious privacy impactions. For instance, firewall logs may contain information about caller identity, frequency, and duration; information about which pay-per-view movie or event was consumed and when it was consumed; when the individual entered and left the physical security perimeter; when they did on-line banking and who they bank with. Taken as a data-set and mined, logs files from converged ICT assets could exposure a very large amount of personal information. Typically, these logs are not treated as sensitive personal information but rather as organizational security artefacts. If logs are protected, it is usually for the purposes of potential forensic evidence. Nobody thinks about infrastructure logs as sources of personal information. As a result, most security controls around logs are aimed at preventing the unauthorized alternation or removal of log data, not viewing or copying.

Convergence transforms the issue around log-management from a banal to a significant issue worthy of management consideration. Logged information about converged assets will become available to people such as network administrators who may have no training in privacy issues and no "need-to-know" for security purposes because it is not their mandate. Consider the privacy impact of a love-sick technical staff member deciding to find out what they can about the good looking HR lady. Or the LAN administrator who takes a dislike to the boss and decides to compile a detailed dossier of all the personal communications transactions she undertakes in a month for delivery to the CEO. Perhaps the administrator also decides to alter the logs (which may be undetectable if there are no safeguards in place) to spice them up a little for the CEO. As the risk matrix to follow demonstrates, it is the cumulative impact of convergence that makes privacy a management concern. These issues did not surface prior to convergence.

VOIP introduces a whole new depth and breath to the "traditional" privacy concerns around data. Call logs, connections, durations, and voicemail records are all records that will be contained within logs of infrastructure components—and not just VOIP infrastructure components, but other more mundane security devices like firewalls. All of a sudden, personal information (such as calling patterns) are contained in the firewall logs along with web traffic and email traffic. These logs are typically managed by, or at least accessible to, a wide range of different people with different roles in organizations. These logs are also backed-up and stored using processes not generally designed to support privacy requirements. In the end, the introduction of voice services onto the IP network inadvertently induce regulatory breach in the following areas:

- Collection of personal information without (at least explicit) consent
- Collection of information without specified purpose
- Availability of personal information to people without need-to-know
- Retention beyond the period legitimately required

When these same issues are extended to logs and account information related to other converged assets like media and entertainment consumption, physical security, metering data, and financial transaction data it becomes apparent that a person's entire life can be reconstructed: personal habits, interests, preferences, foibles, spending patterns, friends, family, productivity.

Contributing to the issues around ICT convergence and privacy is the matter of the enablement of inter-working of devices across distinct network types. The network is becoming transparent to the device and application: WiFi, cellular, ethernet over fiber, DSL, or cable modem. Devices seamlessly "jump" from network to network depending on which is offering better service. The advent of these capabilities will generate issues around the ownership of user profile information and the exchange of user profile information between network operators for billing and accounting. For example, user billing and profile information from DSL users may need to be shared with mobile operators in order to facilitate session "handover" as the subscriber moves from a fixed line network to a cellular network in an automated hand-over. The user may not even be aware the hand-off has occurred or that a third party may be provided partial or full access to their account information. (See "Perimeter Stress" and "Fixed Mobile Union" further in this chapter for more discussion.)

Privacy regulations introduce a potential booby trap into ICT convergence where the intent of logging and record keeping (service-management and transparent accounting) could foster regulatory breaches—what started legitimately ends illegally. Convergence provides easy access to potentially all information flows within an organization. This information can be stored, sorted, searched, and archived for a wide variety of reasons, not the least of which may be regulatory records-management requirements. But once we have access to these data, what are the new applications to which we will want to apply to these data? And how legal will these applications be?

Lawful Access / Communication Assistance to Law Enforcement Agencies (CALEA)

Lawful access to ICT information has always been a serious matter, but is a particular concern in this day and age. Lawful access requires not only that records and information be available, but that there be assurance associated with the information. It is not an overstatement to say that ICT convergence dramatically increases the resources required, and difficulty associated with, managing lawful access.

For instance, VOIP introduces a whole new depth and breath to the traditional wiretap requirements. Entire days worth of conversations can be relatively easily stored and later monitored. Similarly, physical security records (like CCTV, access/entry/exit logs, and burglar alarms) are often transported and stored digitally and may even contain audio; these could prove crucial during criminal investigations. Ultimately, as pointed out in the previous privacy discussion, a very detailed profile of either a business's or individual's activities could be assembled from analysis of converged IP application traffic and/or logs.

That is good news for law enforcement. The bad news is that such access and analysis can amount to a tremendous, if not (currently) impossible task. Consider a few examples around the impact of ICT CALEA.

VOIP Wire Tap Requests

Such requests are routine in the legal world of telephony and well understood. In the VOIP world, with the cooperation of the VOIP service provider (the entity that controls the call manager or media gateway, for instance), wire tapping is viable. However, it is likely that such instances will prove the exception and not the rule, and Law Enforcement Agencies (LEAs) are more likely to encounter situations where significant obstacles for VOIP wiretap exist:

- "Hell's Bells," as they are known in the telecom world, are fly-by-night VOIP service providers that crop-up using public domain VOIP management software and offer cut-rate long-distance service over the public Internet to specific destinations (China, for example). They are known to be frequently non-responsive to lawful access requests and will simply fold their tents and leave rather than expend the resources to comply to LEA requests.[22]
- A small VOIP service provider refuses to comply with LEA requests or simply vanishes, the LEA will approach the upper-level carrier with the request. This is frequently the core-network provider who has sold bandwidth to a smaller Tier-2 or even Tier-3 ISP. Since

---

[22] David Elder meeting, Bell Canada VP Regulatory, May 26, 2005.

the core network does not own or operate any of the VOIP infrastructure, they would be required to essentially intercept all data from the ISP's pipe and sift through it looking for VOIP traffic and the particular VOIP session. Assuming that the provider has this capability, they would then need to archive all the traffic, re-assemble the packets, and de-code the audio stream. This is no mean feat.

- VOIP transport security, when implemented, can pose almost insurmountable obstacles to CALEA compliance because point-to-point encryption can be applied to the voice data stream. This encryption is generally based upon keys negotiated between the client devices and not accessible to either the service provider or the LEA. One potential solution is to implement man-in-the-middle (MITM) analysis capabilities with the collusion of the service providers; however, this will require that the responsible carrier has access to all potential combinations of algorithms and protocol implementations that might be in use by the end-point devices. Also, because of the speed with which a MITM intercept must occur (delay cannot exceed 150 ms end-to-end for VOIP without becoming obvious), hardware implementation of crypto will probably be required.[23] For end-point soft-phones that might be able to change algorithms between calls or even implement proprietary algorithms, hardware crypto becomes a challenge too.

The bottom line with lawful access requests around VOIP is that it is a hotly contested issue for the reasons mentioned above, to name a few.

While the debate about technical requirements, resources, and who pays for what is on-going at this time, non-service provider organizations should pay attention lest they find that LEAs make lawful access requests concerning converged asset traffic or logs which remain within the organization (Walled Garden), in which case the organization itself is the service-provider.

Any user of converged ICT, whether it be Triple Play applications and services or Transparent applications and services, should consider the potential for lawful access requests to logs and information streams from just about any application because of the potential to mine this information for profiling and analysis.

---

[23] Security Challenges for CALEA in Voice over Packet Networks, Sophia Scoggins, Texas Instruments, April 2004.

Asset	Agent/Event	Class of Threat	Threat Assessment				Risk Assessment		
			Likelihood	Consequences of Occurrence	Impact	Exposure Rating	Existing Safeguards	Vulnerabilities	Risk
Data		Confidentiality Integrity Availability	High	Data exposure, corruption, loss	Grave	9	Many well-understood application	Privacy breach, records loss	Medium
VOIP	• Records retention • Privacy • Lawful access	Confidentiality Integrity Availability	High	Data exposure, corruption, loss	Grave	9	Ad hoc extension of data safeguards	Privacy breach, records loss, inability to fulfill lawful access requests	High
Entertainment and Media		Confidentiality Integrity Availability	High	Data exposure, corruption, loss	Serious	8	Ad hoc extension of data safeguards	Privacy breach, records loss, inability to fulfill lawful access requests	Medium
Physical		Confidentiality Integrity Availability	High	Data exposure, corruption, loss	Grave	9	Ad hoc extension of data safeguards	Privacy breach, records loss, inability to fulfill lawful access requests	High

SCADA	Integrity Availability	High	Data exposure, corruption, loss	Moderate	6	Ad hoc extension of data safeguards	Records loss	Low
Banking	Confidentiality Integrity Availability	High	Data exposure, corruption, loss	Grave	9	Dedicated infrastructure, issues well understood from previous technologies	Privacy breach, records loss, inability to fulfill lawful access requests	Medium
Facilities	Integrity Availability	High	Data exposure, corruption, loss	Moderate	6	Ad hoc extension of data safeguards	Records loss	Low
Metering	Confidentiality Integrity Availability	High	Data exposure, corruption, loss	Grave	9	Ad hoc extension of data safeguards	Privacy breach, records loss, inability to fulfill lawful access requests	High

OPERATIONAL THREATS

Operational threats are threats that involve of mechanisms primarily implemented and executed by people (as opposed to systems). These threats may impact individual systems, applications, and processes, or entire groups of systems, applications, and processes. They often derive from a lack of the required technical expertise or as a result of management lapses.

Note: All risk assessments are intended purely to be estimates against the vulnerabilities in a fictitious organization that has adopted converged systems without really understanding the impacts. The safeguards described are merely the typical, native safeguards of a given asset. Organizations need to consider these assessments in light of the actual safeguards in place in their distinct organizations and apply their own risk assessment process.

Location-Implied Functionality

A critical element of the functionality of many assets is related to knowledge of their physical location and, therefore, the location from which the data originates. Location-implied functionality refers to the assumptions around physical location of an asset and the information/logs/metrics arriving from that asset. For instance, a phone located at a known street address, a thermostat in a specific room, a meter on a specific client-site.

Location-implied functionality can no longer be taken for granted, as it has been in the past with devices using dedicated (un-convergent) networks. For instance 911 functions rely upon the location of the phone being known, and break down on routed IP networks because 911 calls from VOIP phones can literally come from anywhere in the world.[24] Similarly, devices used for monitoring physical locations (like doors) or physical processes (like oil well–heads) may appear to be fully functional but the information

---

[24] NIST 800–58, pg 7.

which supports this conclusion could be forged, impersonated, or replayed from a hostile device with the ability to tap the network.

The assurance of many ICT assets relies upon location-based functionality, and assumes the physical location of the device is known and unchanged. The only asset to which this is not a new consideration or threat is Internet data, which has "grown up" on IP and the absence of locational assurance.

Location-Implied Functionality

Asset	Agent/Event	Threat Assessment					Risk Assessment		
		Class of Threat	Likelihood	Consequences of Occurrence	Impact	Exposure Rating	Existing Safeguards	Vulnerabilities	Risk
Data		NA	NA	NA	NA	NA	NA	NA	NA
VOIP		Integrity	High	911 dependant upon caller instructions	Grave	9	None-no technical solution yet available	Emergency services cannot locate caller	High
Entertainment and Media		NA	NA	NA	NA	NA	NA	NA	NA
Physical	• Malicious insider • Negligent insider • Hacker	Integrity	High	Cannot be certain of device information	Grave	9	Limited network security	False alarms, decoy information hides outage	High
SCADA		Integrity	High	Cannot be certain device readings are legitimate	Grave	9	Isolated networks	Decoy information hides outage	Medium
Banking		Integrity	High	Cannot be certain device readings are legitimate	Grave	9	Isolated networks, encryption, device authentication	Decoy information hides outage	Medium
Facilities		Integrity	High	Cannot be certain device readings are legitimate	Grave	9	Limited network security	Decoy information hides outage	High
Metering		Integrity	High	Cannot be certain device readings are legitimate	Grave	9	Limited network security, device authentication	Decoy information hides outage	Medium

Quality of Service (QoS): Only as Good as the Weakest Link

Not all converged assets will be as susceptible to QoS assurance-related issues as others. Some applications are highly sensitive to QoS while other will tolerate significant QoS degradation; however, if all assets are converged, the network QoS must be maintained at the lowest levels tolerated by the most sensitive applications. Planning for and delivering QoS in an internal corporate network is a known and understood technical requirement for certain converged applications like VOIP. However, these plans and provisions are limited to the assets operating within the organizational perimeter. Once converged applications (like VOIP streams) leave the corporate network perimeter for third-party networks, all bets are off. QoS on the open Internet is very different from QoS inside the Walled Garden—it's like the North Atlantic compared to a country lake.

The first consideration around QoS is the processing and management latency introduced by infrastructure associated with the converged assets; accounting systems for Triple Play services, firewall rules, architectural safeguards and VPN-type safeguards. Crypto latency within routers and firewalls supporting VPN can introduce delays because of scheduling algorithms within crypto-engines,[25] degrading any data quality in certain converged applications beyond usability.

"As best practice one will also need to consider that VOIP (and related applications) being real-time communications as they are; are an order of magnitude more sensitive to network disruptions (e.g., one snowballing side effect is you can't dial out or have poor voice quality to notify your administration of poor network performance–to wit). Thus maintaining network behavior is a business continuity requirement."[26]

QoS issues are further complicated by the fact that QoS means different things to different converged assets. Take Call-centers versus SCADA as an example. Call centers often drive the customer

---

[25] R. Barbieri, D. Brushi, "Voice over IPsec: Analysis and Solutions", Proceedings of the 18th Annual Computer Security Applications Conference 2002.
[26] VOIP Security Association mailing list, July 1, 2005 Mani, Mahalingam, mmani@avaya.com.

experience and interface and are a significant if not the major source of sales. Call centers acquire significant savings and efficiencies from VOIP and related Internet communications tools like Chat and Instant Messaging, which means that QoS delays that reduce VOIP performance are a primary concern. Alternately, SCADA applications support critical telemetry and events that must be tracked over time. SCADA may be severely impacted by lost packets and errors but tolerate latency.[27] "Unlike information networks, industrial control networks place a greater burden on the designers of system components. An industrial control network requires fast and guaranteed (*deterministic*) throughput to effectively control machines and manufacturing processes."[28] A converged network supporting both VOIP and SCADA applications (Triple Play plus Transparent convergence) will be a QoS challenge.

Adding to the QoS challenges, traditional countermeasures in the data world of IT security and assurance inhibit the functionality and therefore the value of certain converged assets. This presents a double-edged sword to security architects: employ countermeasures which are tried and true, but degrade or deny newly converged services. A few simple but high relevant examples follow.

- Network address translation (NAT) is a system which has one specific purpose and an excellent security by-product. NAT is intended to allow organizations to have vast internal networks behind a single (or several) routable IP address. This means that an organization's network growth and design is not restricted by how many IP addresses they have been granted either from their ISP or from the Internet Assigned Numbers Authority.[29] The security by-product is that no internal topology information needs to be disclosed to public routers and all traffic can be funneled and filtered through single points of access, i.e., firewalls. Unfortunately, due to the nature of (particularly) VOIP signaling and information flows, NAT does not always allow telephony connections to be established as a security by-product.[30] (VOIP with SIP or H.323 as the signaling

---

[27] A practical Guide to Transforming your Call Centre with IP technology, CMP Media Call Centre Group, 2005.

[28] Ethernet: Surviving the Manufacturing Environment White Paper, Bob Lousnbury, Physical Layer Engineer, Rockwell Automation, May 2001.

[29] http://www.iana.org.

[30] NIST 800-58 pg Chapter 7, pg 52.

protocols uses a wide number of ports, with the signaling portion of the connection being distinct from the audio connections. The affect is that signaling triggers network connections that appear unrelated and potentially dangerous to "naive" NAT routers. Allowing external connections to be initiated from outside the internal network to a multitude of dynamic points within the internal network can be very dangerous.) Additionally, NAT may introduce latency that has critical performance impacts on converged applications, as the NAT device tries to juggle dozens of connections for just a small number of actual calls.

- IPSec or Virtual Private Network (VPN) technology is another tried and true security counter-measure that can have negative impacts on converged applications. IPSec or a VPN might be implemented in situations where remote offices are linked over shared network from ISPs. Or an IPSec connection might be used on an internal network to segregate especially sensitive information from the rest of the corporate network traffic. However, cryptographic features applied to IP packets will increase their size and therefore the resource required to transport them. In the case of VOIP, IPSec increases the size of the UDP VOIP packet by as much as 63%.[31] The result is a very significant increase in network traffic loads and the QoS issues described above come into play.

- Potentially independent of the IPSec example is the use of strong authentication technologies for mission critical information flows. Such authentication may involve a variety of different challenge-response techniques and/or public-key based hand-shakes, but in all cases will require several additional network transactions and exchanges in order to establish credentials and authentication between the devices. This again represents a double-edged sword for those trying to provide assurance to converged networks and assets using traditional safeguards taken from the "data-only world": establishing strong authentication requires connection set-up latency that could make delays too long for frequent connections/disconnections (like VOIP), or create a vulnerability to

---

[31] C-N. Chuah, "Providing End-to-End QoS for IP based Latency sensitive Applications." Technical Report, Dept. of Electrical Engineering and Computer Science, University of California at Berkeley, 2000.

a very but simple lethal attack designed to force a connection re-set and re-authentication.

QoS must be considered not just from the perspective of speed (latency), but error rates and lost packets. All the metrics associated with these measures must be no lower than the most sensitive converged asset requires. The extension of this conclusion is that factors that might not necessarily be considered in the provisioning of QoS are suddenly more relevant and possibly beyond the scope of the standard QoS engineering that organizations undertake. As an example, industrial settings can generate very elevated noise levels on ethernets which can severely degrade performance. Switches and hubs will filter out collisions related to noise-induced signaling problems but not errors.[32] (See "Electrical Environmental Sensitivity" for further details.)

---

[32] Ethernet: Surviving the Manufacturing Environment White Paper, Bob Lousnbury, Physical Layer Engineer, Rockwell Automation, May 2001.

Quality of Service Only as Good as the Weakest Link

Asset	Threat Assessment					Risk Assessment			
	Agent/Event	Class of Threat	Likelihood	Consequences of Occurrence	Impact	Exposure Rating	Existing Safeguards	Vulnerabilities	Risk
Data	• Network overload • Device-induced latency • Crypto-induced latency • Physical environment	Availability	High	Few	Moderate	6	Native TCP/IP error correction and delivery assurance	Few: Data delays measured in seconds	Low
VOIP		Integrity Availability	High	Degradation of voice services	Grave	9	Initial network assessments at install, monitoring	UDP-based service: Slower adoption, reduced ROI and increased costs, voice service collapse	High
Entertainment and Media		Integrity Availability	High	Loss of TV service, unauthorized access to services	Moderate	6	Initial network assessments at install, monitoring	UDP-based service: Slower adoption, reduced ROI and increased costs, service collapse and refunds to clients	High
Physical		Integrity Availability	High	Delay of access to sites, loss of video surveillance	Serious	8	Initial network assessments at install, monitoring	UDP-based service: Employee productivity, physical breaches undetected or suspected	Medium

(Continued)

Quality of Service Only as Good as the Weakest Link (*Continued*)

Asset	Threat Assessment						Risk Assessment		
	Agent/Event	Class of Threat	Likelihood	Consequences of Occurrence	Impact	Exposure Rating	Existing Safeguards	Vulnerabilities	Risk
SCADA		Integrity Availability	High	Loss of control of manufacturing processes	Grave	9	Initial network assessments at install, monitoring	Undetected faults and flaws in production	High
Banking		Integrity Availability	High	Unable to execute transactions	Grave	9	Native TCP/IP error correction and delivery assurance, device caching of transaction data	Few: Transaction delays in seconds are normal	Low
Facilities		Integrity Availability	High	Loss of control of lighting, heating, cooling	Serious	8	Native TCP/IP error correction and delivery assurance	Few: Delays in seconds	Low
Metering		Integrity Availability	High	Loss of remote control of devices, falsification of data	Grave	9	Native TCP/IP error correction and delivery assurance	Few: delays in seconds	Low

Perimeter Stress

There are countervailing forces at work when it comes to converged network perimeter-assurance and the way in which it must be managed. These forces ratchet up stress between those trying to draw further efficiencies and returns from the network and those trying to secure the network. The forces generating this stress are: a) the growth in outsourced support and third-party managed services, which require more and more entry points into the network; and b) the increasing requirement for assurance. Outsourcing and remote support and management drive the requirement for remote access to enable outsourcing savings and efficiencies. The more devices and services that are converged onto the network, the more business demands there are for remote access capabilities to the one common network, and the more legitimate requirements to access the network from an ever wider variety of entry points. This leads to more modems and dedicated connections from third parties such as suppliers, contractors, and customers. The result is multiple entry points behind the firewall and likely across all network segments for very different but potentially valid reasons.

While these sorts of relationships and requirements for remote access are not new, convergence significantly changes the nature of this requirement. Previously, the remote access was being granted to isolated and independent networks or, in some cases, independent devices. Under IP convergence, all these devices and services are on the IP network and all remote access will be to the same physical network. Once access has been gained to the physical network, it is a simple matter to access information traveling over that common physical medium. As an example, an organization may have had requirements for remote access to the data network, the phones network, the HVAC system, and the burglar alarms system for remote administration. This represented a total of four "back doors" to the organizations, but they all went to mutually exclusive destinations. Under convergence, this may represent four different backdoors to the same IP network with completely different access controls and safeguards.

As organizational ICT assets converge on IP, perimeter stresses will increase significantly as the demands associated with allowing entry through the "secure perimeter" become overwhelming for all but the most empowered and self-assured security managers.

Another form of perimeter stress is the number of configurations and holes that have to be punched in the firewalls to support certain converged applications if they originate, or are intended to support communications outside the organizational wide area network (WAN). VOIP, depending on which protocols are employed, will utilize anywhere from 3 to 11 ports, most of which are dynamic. For instance, H.323 will use between 7 and 11 ports with only 2 static ports; SIP will use at least 3 ports with only 1 being static.[33] This poses an enormous challenge to both firewalls and firewall administrators, which can easily result in both technical and human failures.

Another example of stress may be the collection of metering data from remote sources over an IP network that touches thousands or even millions of remote, uncontrolled locations (like residential housing or car parking). The firewalls in this instance may be required to manage large volumes of proprietary industrial protocols which have no form of application-level filtering available because the protocols are not supported by any firewall vendor. In this case, administrators may be forced to allow all traffic through specified ports (general service ports), which means that external attackers can simply channel attacks through this one naive port, undetected. Firewall vendor selection may become a narrow competition based upon which communications protocols are supported by application-level proxies, relieving organizations of the requirement to use general service ports.

Firewalls can also become overloaded supporting VOIP and trying to maintain a vast number of opening and closing ports and trying to track the states of these ports to prevent externally mounted attacks like Spam over Internet Telephony (SPIT) attacks. On the human side, the requirement to manage a complex rule set on a large number of firewalls will likely result in operator errors such as mis-configuration or mistakes around patch management, all leading to a compromise of the fundamental perimeter defenses.

A final form of perimeter stress revolves around bandwidth availability coupled with the adoption of converged applications in an organization and how it may lead to fatal, ad hoc network upgrades. This matter is in line with the more general notion of supporting too many routes into the network. Bandwidth availability can occur in either physical or logical ways. Physically, it

---

[33] IP Telephony Security, MetaGroup Whitepaper, January 2005, pg 4.

can result from mere lack of fixed-line network cabling into a particular office space or location for any number of reasons (e.g., cost, distance, architecture), or perhaps assurance requirements for a given network segment will not allow certain types of users and applications to utilize the physical transport. Logically, bandwidth availability issues can derive from too many users and/or applications on a given network segment. In either case, stress will be placed on the network managers to extend the network cheaply and quickly.

In organizations that have not undertaken or are just starting the process of asset convergence, some questions often come up: Do we need to extend more than one network? Is it necessary to run independent cabling for data, voice, physical security and facilities management? Can we run a single physical network supporting all IP assets? The answer—run one IP network, of course! Under current thinking, this is virtually a given outcome. The extenuating impact of this single-network philosophy is that the same physical network is constantly being extended in all directions to support all assets. Every time one of the three varieties of Triple Play assets or of the five varieties of Transparent assets require extension of the network infrastructure, all assets ride along.

Two issues result from this sort approach to extending (and therefore stressing) the perimeter network:

First, the sensitivity of the converged IP network requires that network extensions do not happen ad hoc. Period. Second, careful attention needs to be paid to the physical transport medium selected. Often in situations where new cabling is problematic, alternatives are sought. A couple of alternatives to regular CAT-5 ethernet cable are wireless connections and ethernet over in-building powerline.[34] Both these solutions have been shown to support converged ICT applications and assets and have variable and potentially unpredictable impacts on ICT assurance due to signal leakage and the introduction of unauthorized devices. Ethernet over powerline is currently a niche technology and probably not likely to grow substantially, if for no other reason than that alternative technology like CAT-5, fiber, co-axial and wireless are already incumbent and improving their capabilities daily. Powerline technology will

---

[34] Current Technologies, http://www.currenttechnologies.com/solutions/voip.html.

probably never catch-up or keep up. Wireless, on the other hand, warrants further discussion.

Fixed-Mobile Union

Fixed Mobile Union (FMU) is the phenomenon whereby the distinct wireless and fixed-line networks merge into one network as far as the ICT users, devices, and assets are concerned. The network with the best performance or availability is automatically selected by devices. FMU is the technical integration of traditionally fixed-line networks [e.g., CAT-5, co-axial, fiber, unshielded twisted pair-(UTP)] and mobile/wireless networks (GSM and CDMA, WiFi/802.11, WiMax/802.16, and 3G Cellular units) in a way that allows the services to operate "seamlessly" across network boundaries, maintaining IP session persistence and authentication as the user moves from one access network to another. From the perspective of users and assets, there is only one network. Confusingly, this is sometimes also referred to as "fixed mobile convergence"—yet another "convergence."

The element of FMU that will increase perimeter stress in the near future and change the approach to building and operating ICT networks is IMS (IP Multimedia Subsystem). IMS is the architecture for Third Generation Mobile Networks defined by the 3GPP (Third Generation Partnership Project), a consortium of GSM carriers and equipment, device, and technology vendors. IMS provides the normalized architecture for the third generation of mobile communications (3G) mobile network core. [The first generation was analogue cellular; the second generation was digital PCS (IE. GSM and CDMA) services.] The standard was first defined in Third Generation Partnership Project (3GPP) release 5, which was ratified in November 2003. Release 6, ratified one year later, added important new functionality, including interworking with WiFi. 3GPP provides standards for building an all-IP core network that allows the provision of any IP application across any access network [Cellular, 3G, WiFi (IEEE 802.11), WiMax (IEEE 802.16), Cable Modem, DSL, etc.] to any end point device. These new services will require unprecedented cooperation among mobile, fixed, and enterprise network operators to ensure security and quality of service. Because it defines a common set of standard interfaces among access networks, transports, and applications, IMS is seen by many network experts as a key enabler of FMU. IMS will also make the control of the network perimeter even more difficult because the ability of devices to transparently hop from one network to another distinct network is facilitated. Part of the unintended benefits of our current "primitive" IP networks is that movement from one network to another is rarely transparent; devices (to the benefit of assurance) do not function without use intervention providing a last ware of defence.

IMS is access network agnostic, thereby greatly reducing or eliminating the development work that must be done to deploy a given IP application over a new access network. In today's telecom networks the interfaces between applications and the underlying transport network are typically tightly coupled and proprietary. IMS removes the dependency between the application and the underlying transport network, and uses common open standards interfaces between the application and transport layers, thereby dramatically increasing the available pool of application developers who can build applications for IMS.

IMS de-couples applications from dependency on the physical medium of transport. To an application (such as Data, Voice, Entertainment and Media, Metering, Scada, etc.), a network is a network. IMS separates transport, control, and application functions into separate layers, and defines the interfaces between these layers and well as the interface between functions within each of these layers.

IMS is designed to support real-time multimedia services by including the use of Session Initiation Protocol (SIP). 3GPP added additional extensions to IETF SIP to provide for Security, QoS, charging, and Mobility Management (i.e., the ability to handover a call or session as the user device moves from one access network or cell to another). The combination of these well-defined interfaces and the inclusion of SIP to support real-time services provide a strong foundation for wireless and wireline carriers to deploy an entirely new class of services that allows the "blending" of applications such as Push to Talk (PTT) and photo or image sharing.

IMS is peer-to-peer focused and leverages the power of IP to provide one-to-many communications. This means primarily that the focus will be on applications that enhance person-to-person communications.

Key security considerations that emerge with FMU and IMS include:

1. Defining a common means of Authentication Authorization and Accounting/Billing (AAA) between wireless and fixed-line network perimeters. IMS defines Diameter as the standard, while

most enterprises currently use RADIUS- and GSM cellular networks use SIM-based methods.

2. Defining standard means of security and remote management on mobile devices. IMS does not define encryption standards or remote management capability, but leverages IEEE Standards such as 802.1i for non-cellular network security.

3. Extending authentication mid-session to allow for session "hand-over" as the user moves between access networks (e.g., from WiFi to DSL or cellular). The effect may be to allow devices not authenticated by the organization inside the perimeter based upon a third-party authentication.

4. Potential new vulnerabilities such as signaling and other messages (SMS, MMS, etc.) from trusted cellular networks are delivered into unlicensed (WiFi primarily) public and enterprise networks, where network controls are more difficult to enforce.

5. The vulnerabilities related to cellular signaling entering fixed line networks is largely unexplored. It is known from VOIP experience that the SS7 to IP gateways can become conduits for denial of service attacks. Cellular phone number ranges assigned to carriers by regulatory agencies are publicly available. When malicious entities sequentially combine number-blocks with the carriers public domain names (555–1234 @telco.com), it becomes straightforward to launch indiscriminate attacks against the carrier and organizational messaging infrastructure.

Extension of converged ICT networks represents a serious threat to organizations and must be a controlled and carefully considered process, not left to low-level administrators or third-party installers.

Perimeter Stress

Asset	Threat Assessment						Risk Assessment		
	Agent/Event	Class of Threat	Likelihood	Consequences of Occurrence	Impact	Exposure Rating	Existing Safeguards	Vulnerabilities	Risk
Data	• Multiple un-rationalized access points to network • Malicious external entities	Confidentiality Integrity Availability	High	Compromise of systems and infrastructure	Grave	9	Mature protocols and application level firewalls, LAN access control technologies, network IDS	Eavesdropping and interception of data, malicious attacks on assets/denial of service, regulatory breach	High
VOIP	• Uncontrolled extension of the perimeter • Fixed mobile union	Confidentiality Integrity Availability	High	Lost intellectual property, lost productivity, infrastructure compromise	Grave	9	LAN access control technologies, network IDS	Eavesdropping and interception of data, malicious attacks on assets/denial of service	High
Entertainment and Media		Confidentiality Integrity Availability	High	Loss of TV service, unauthorized access to services, infrastructure compromise	Serious	8	LAN access control Technologies, network IDS	Malicious attacks on assets/denial of service	Medium
Physical		Confidentiality Integrity Availability	High	Delay of access to sites, loss of video surveillance, system compromise, infrastructure compromise	Grave	9	LAN access control Technologies, network IDS	Malicious attacks on assets/denial of service	High

(Continued)

Perimeter Stress (Continued)

Asset	Agent/Event	Threat Assessment						Risk Assessment		
		Class of Threat	Likelihood	Consequences of Occurrence	Impact	Exposure Rating	Existing Safeguards	Vulnerabilities	Risk
SCADA		Confidentiality Integrity Availability	High	Loss of control of manufacturing processes, infrastructure compromise	Grave	9	LAN access control technologies, network IDS	Malicious attacks on assets/denial of service	High
Banking		Confidentiality Integrity Availability	High	Transactions unable to execute, infrastructure compromise	Grave	9	LAN access control technologies, network IDS, devices VPN and session security	Malicious attacks on assets/denial of service	High
Facilities		Confidentiality Integrity Availability	High	Loss of control of lighting, heating, cooling; infrastructure compromise	Grave	9	LAN access control technologies, network IDS	Malicious attacks onassets/denial of service	High
Metering		Confidentiality Integrity Availability	High	Loss of remote control of devices, falsification of data infrastructure compromise	Grave	9	LAN access control technologies, network IDS	Malicious attacks on assets/denial of service	High

Technical Threats

Technical threat involve the potential for automated or remote exploitation of network devices, protocols, or computer systems. These threats may derive from either malicious or benign sources and activities, unplanned or unauthorized changes, or the introduction of new devices into the infrastructure. Technical threats may also arise from authorized or planned changes that are not tested thoroughly.

Note: All risk assessments are intended to be estimates against the vulnerabilities in a fictitious organization which has adopted converged systems without really understanding the impacts. The safeguards described are merely the typical, native safeguards of a given asset. Organizations need to consider these assessments in light of the actual safeguards in place in their distinct organizations and apply their own risk assessment process.

Electrical Environment Sensitivity

The electrical environment of IP networks is a well-understood technical threat that takes on a new meaning under convergence. All the standard physical environment issues apply as before; water precautions, cooling/heating controls, and humidity are all as important as ever. But the threats around the electrical environment are both heightened and in some cases new, requiring a fresh look by managers coping with the assurance of converged networks.

Reliance on uninterrupted power supply (UPS) is heightened significantly because previously isolated networks with independent power sources are now dependant on the same IP network: If your network loses power, you lose your data, your phones, your process control, your physical security, etc. These IP networks all contain multiple, remote in-line devices such as routers, hubs, and switches, the failure of which would result in network bottlenecks at best or network failure at worst. In-line devices are so common and dispersed throughout organizations that the prospect of providing all of them with any sort of even rudimentary UPS is a large expense, often requiring major modifications to physical infrastructure such as wiring and telecom closets, which were not designed for the storage of UPS batteries. Further, UPS devices are really low-tech batteries, and require frequent inspection and maintenance to remain reliable and to preserve the assurance of the network. Such inspections further increase the cost and/or risks of converged IP networks.

This equates to the emergence of a new aggregated threat related to electrical systems, which is especially evident when considering the convergence of voice onto IP. The dial-tone is now dependant on the routers, switches, and firewalls. Previously, telephony would be powered using 48 volts of power coming over the telephone line itself and supplied by the telco[35] or though the office PBX, which would likely be engineered with sufficient UPS to keep the phones functional during power failures.

The quality of service and availability we have come to expect from voice services is inherently related to the means by which these services were traditionally powered, i.e., a distinct power source from the one feeding the structure in which the phones were located. Depending upon the manufacturer, many facilities management components from thermostats to smoke detectors are powered in the same manner—low voltage supplied through a shielded wire within the wiring bundle.

Another lesser known, but potent, electrical threat to IP networks concerns electromagnetic "noise" at the physical level of the network.[36] The potential for electronic noise to disrupt network signals is well known, and is accounted for in standard LAN cabling through shielding of the wires. This shielding is effective in a wide range of environments and is available in different gradients of shielding that relate to environmental factors such as heat, cold, vibration, humidity, UV exposure and various forms of electromagnetic interference.

Some environments are also more electrically punitive than others: "[Ethernet] products must be designed to withstand the electrical and mechanical noises produced by a plant's floor equipment. These types of noises range from EMI generated by contact arcing and welding processes to RF fields from high power sources like radio transmitters.... Historically, control equipment and industrial networks have been designed to survive electromagnetic compatibility (EMC) directives as defined by the European Communities. In addition, products must conform to other local agency requirements such as Under Writers Laboratories, C-TECK and Federal Communications Commission (FCC). The objective of these

---

[35] NIST 800–58 pg 24.

[36] Ethernet: Surviving the Manufacturing Environment White Paper, Bob Lounsbury, Physical Layer Engineer, Rockwell Automation, May 2001.

Sources of Industrial Noises[36]		
Type	**Noise**	**Coupling Mechanism**
Electric motors	Surge and EFT[*]	Local ground, conducted
Drive controllers	Conducted and surge	Local ground, conducted
Relays and contactors	EFT	Radiated, conducted
Welding	EFT, induction	Radiated, magnetic
RF induction welding	Radio frequency	Radiated, conducted
Material handling paper/textile	ESD[**]	Radiated
Heating	EFT	Local ground, conducted, radiated
Induction heating	EFT	Local ground, conducted, radiated
Radio communications	Radio frequency	Radiated

[*]EFT (Electrical Fast Transient): Line disturbances caused by switching transients from nearby relays, motors, and other switched devices.
[**]ESD (Electro Static Discharge): The transfer of charge between bodies at different electrical potentials. High levels of ESD may upset the operation of an electronic system, causing equipment malfunction or failure.

directives is to protect from external electromagnetic interference (EMI) and to limit electromagnetic emissions. In other words, products should be designed to withstand external noise and limit potentially disruptive noise emissions..." Therefore, the problem comes when IP networks designed for normal data requirements are then extended into industrial environments for purposes related to Transparent convergence and assets.

"For an office system, latency caused by link errors may go unnoticed. However, in a control system, link errors may lead to jitter which may be unacceptable in some machine or process control applications."

"The effects of worst-case impedance and capacitance unbalanced, coupled with the effects of temperature, can degrade [ethernet] system performance by anywhere from 7–14%." While regular LAN and WAN routers and switches would filter out much of this noise and prevent the SCADA components of the converged networks from fouling the business segments with noise, having two significant affects:

1. Errors caused by electromagnetic interference on the network will still be passed back to the business segments and generate loads even if router and switches filter out pure noise.
2. Applications that must receive configuration or operation instructions over this network may frequently fail to receive all instructions. And if these devices are relying on UDP for real-time delivery of information, the loss of these instruction sets or telemetry will not be detected by the device of the network, leaving operators and applications to try and put the pieces together.

Electrical Environment Sensitivity

Asset	Threat Assessment						Risk Assessment		
	Agent/Event	Class of Threat	Likelihood	Consequences of Occurrence	Impact	Exposure Rating	Existing Safeguards	Vulnerabilities	Risk
Data	• Power failure • Electromagnetic interference	Integrity Availability	High	Data services out. No email, web, directory or VPN access	Grave	9	UPS of central services and customer-facing resources	Loss of email, web, database, back-office systems. Unable to support customers	Medium
VOIP		Integrity Availability	High	Loss of voice services	Grave	9	UPS on VOIP infrastructure components	No 911 services, No voice services to fall back on after data failure	High
Entertainment and Media		Integrity Availability	High	Loss of TV service	Grave	9	UPS of Entertainment and Media infrastructure components	Loss of billable services	Medium
Physical		Integrity Availability	High	Loss of control of physical security, loss of access-events (logs)	Grave	9	Device caches, UPS on central infrastructure components	Unauthorized access to facilities. Undetected physical threats like fire, burglar alarms	High

(Continued)

Electrical Environment Sensitivity (*Continued*)

Asset	Agent/Event	Threat Assessment						Risk Assessment		
		Class of Threat	Likelihood	Consequences of Occurrence	Impact	Exposure Rating	Existing Safeguards	Vulnerabilities	Risk
SCADA		Integrity Availability	High	Loss of control of manufacturing processes	Grave	9	Device caches, UPS on central infrastructure components	Telemetry lost, damage to equipment, lost production, physical safety of staff	High
Banking		Integrity Availability	High	Transactions unable to execute	Grave	9	Device caches, UPS on central infrastructure components, use cash	Regulatory breach	Medium
Facilities		Integrity Availability	High	Loss of control of lighting, heating, cooling	Grave	9	UPS on central infrastructure components	Evacuation of facilities, loss of ability to conduct business	High
Metering		Integrity Availability	High	Loss of remote control of devices	Grave	9	Device caches, UPS on central infrastructure components, use cash	Unable to bill/invoice for services	Medium

Soft Devices: Talented Mimics

Soft devices are software programs that utilize the native processing power of host computer to mimic the functionality of "hard devices." Soft devices typically run on standard platforms like PC devices or laptops. Through soft devices (such as a VOIP phone) it becomes possible to accidentally or deliberately trigger a malfunction or denial-of-service (DoS) on just about any converged service through the attempts of an unauthorized soft device to utilize the service. Similarly, soft devices could be employed to undertake forms of attack such as recording then replaying data streams in order to simulate the functioning of a legitimate hard device. It is also possible for a malicious soft device to inject information intended to simulate a functioning (local) device from anywhere in the world—and IP will faithfully route it and deliver the information.

While there are plenty of ways to detect and prevent the mimicking of hard-devices by illicit software devices, most such countermeasures have not been incorporated into the infrastructures supporting converged applications. For instance, checking source IP addresses, MAC addresses, time-stamps, or even digital signatures are generally well beyond the intended functionality of many converged infrastructures, even though such countermeasures have become second nature to Data (Internet) devices and the related security practices.

Alternately, a soft device could simply acquire access to converged assets through the LAN and use them illicitly; for instance, soft-phones or television software on desktops could engage in theft of service, toll fraud, or digital rights infringements from corporate locations using corporate assets.

To a certain extent, the converged assets newly arrived on IP are "babes in the woods," with predictable vulnerabilities that soft devices will be able to exploit.

Soft Devices: Talented Mimics

Asset	Agent/Event	Threat Assessment					Risk Assessment		
		Class of Threat	Likelihood	Consequences of Occurrence	Impact	Exposure Rating	Existing Safeguards	Vulnerabilities	Risk
Data	• Unauthorized insider • Malicious insider • Hacker • Sabotage	NA	NA	NA	NA	NA	NA	NA	NA
VOIP		Integrity Availability	High	Loss of voice services, unauthorized access to services	Grave	9	None of significance	Theft of service, denial of service	High
Entertainment and Media		Availability	High	Loss of TV service, unauthorized access to services	Moderate	6	None of significance	Theft of service, denial of service	Medium
Physical		Integrity Availability	High	Loss of control of physical security, falsification of control records	Grave	9	None of significance	False alarms, denial of service	High
SCADA		Integrity Availability	High	Loss of control of manufacturing processes, falsification of control records	Grave	9	Physically distinct LAN separated by firewall from data network	False telemetry corrupts control processes, damage to equipment, lost production, physical safety of staff	Medium

Banking	Integrity Availability	High	Transactions unable to execute, falsification of transactions	Grave	9	Physically distinct network, encryption/ authentication on all end-points	Regulatory breach	Low
Facilities	Integrity Availability	High	Loss of control of lighting, heating, cooling	Serious	8	None of significance	Evacuation of facilities, loss of ability to conduct business	High
Metering	Integrity Availability	High	Loss of remote control of devices, falsification of data	Grave	9	Physically distinct LAN separated by firewall from data network	Unable to bill/ invoice for services	Medium

Green Protocols, Stacks, and Architectures

Many newly converged applications and assets are being exposed to the perils of the IP (Internet) world without the benefit of having grown up in this hostile, threat-rich environment. Typically, they possess implementation flaws that threaten not only the asset itself, but the assurance of the converged network as a whole. These flaws exist in two primary forms: 1) outright *protocol implementation weaknesses and flaws*, or 2) implementation of otherwise robust protocols in such a *poor architectural* manner that they threaten other assets sharing the network. Combine these two vulnerabilities within a single element and the chances of asset compromise are significant.

First, let's address protocol implementation flaws, starting with VOIP. Standards for VOIP in particular are not settled and vendors have been implementing quickly in a rush to market. As a result, many VOIP components support multiple protocols for the same purposes. And to date, all the implementations of these protocols are prone to flaws and vulnerabilities from vendor to vendor. Maintaining patches could become onerous very quickly and unpatched systems represent some of the most serious vulnerabilities in ICT systems. In order to not be prescriptive and be competitive, VOIP equipment manufacturers are frequently in the position of supporting multiple competing protocols within a single product, for instance:

a. SIP and H.323 (competitive signaling protocols)
b. MCGP and H.248 (competitive signaling protocols)
c. Vendor specific protocols
d. RTP and RTMP
e. IAX (from the public domain IP PBX "Asterik"[37]).

This type of complexity has led to a specialized industry of "stack vendors." Stack vendors sell "ready made" implementations of these protocols to VOIP (or other converged application) vendors who want to concentrate on the application not the networking stack. When flaws in these OEM stacks are discovered, they can impact dozens of vendors at the same time. The use of stack vendors has become increasingly common as niche equipment manufacturers attempt to enter Greenfield equipment markets quickly.

---

[37] http://www.asterisk.org/about.

Protocol implementation flaws lead to protocol vulnerabilities. SIP, like LDAP was for directory vendors before it, was not always implemented by equipment vendors in a complete manner, which makes it vulnerable to attacks using the simplest scripting tools. A prime example of these tools is contained within the PROTOS test suite for SIP from the University of Oulo, Finland. Oulo is both renowned and notorious for this sort of thing.[38] On one hand they publicize important vulnerability information and give manufacturers fair warning before they make announcements; on the other hand, they basically enable "script-kiddies" with tools to bring down critical systems that have not been patched. The SIP test dates from December 2003 at which time vendors were advised of the results[39]; it is hoped that the vendors have since addressed these issues in subsequent releases.

Related to protocol implementation issues are architectural issues that crop up when converged ICT assets are bolted onto existing technical architectures, making certain assumptions about the assurance of the ICT asset. "We assume X is true because Y is known to be true." A prime example of a new, converged asset impacting the assurance of a technical architecture is in the area of bank card and credit-card activation and authentication. A typical means to activate a new card is to call a 1–800 number and type in the card number. On the back-end, the system matches the number from which you are calling (via caller ID) with the number on record for the card holder. If the numbers match, the card is activated. If the numbers do not match the card holder is simply placed in a queue to speak to a live operator. Under VOIP convergence and especially with the advent of small, third-party service providers, there is less assurance that the telephone number declared in the VOIP signaling information is valid. A moderately skilled fraud artist could change the caller ID information to match whatever they find in the phonebook for the new card they have intercepted. As anyone acquainted with Internet fraud will tell you, on-line criminals are far more than "moderately skilled"—they are professionals.

Digital Rights Management (DRM) tools and software within Triple Play convergence is another area with the potential to cause more harm than good when improperly implemented and managed.

---

[38] http://www.ee.oulu.fi/research/ouspg/protos/testing/c07/sip.
[39] http://www.cert.org/advisories/CA-2003-06.html.

DRM is a very difficult issue to deal with from a technology perspective because it represents an attempt to enforce a condition upon a user that they may rather not submit to: paying for content. On purpose-built devices such CD players or smaller MP3 players, it may be a relatively simple matter to implement DRM within the embedded software of the device. However, DRM abuse is instigated on full-featured computers, and most computers are based upon operating systems to which the user has extensive access and nearly complete control. The potential to circumvent the DRM safeguards is limited only by the design of the DRM tools themselves.

When assessing a threat agent, two factors are generally taken into account to determine the potential severity of the risks: 1) how many resources are at the disposal of the threat agent and 2) how motivated is the agent. Resources can be considered as knowledge, skills, or money. DMR abuse is generally undertaken by a wide range of people and pinning down a typical "abuser profile" would be difficult; however, within this pool of people are those both highly-resourced from a skill perspective, and highly motivated. The motivation varies from person to person but it would be fair to assume that it is a combination of price (paying $1 for a blank CD versus $20 for a fully licensed music CD), plus the immediate availability of the content (no waiting for stores to open or for deliveries), plus the plain thrill of being able to get away with DRM abuse. DRM is confronted with possibly one of the most hostile threat environments concerning any converged asset. An aggregated threat agent that is highly resourced and highly motivated. In the face of this threat agent only the most hardened and well designed DRM tools will survive, and none have yet been devised!

The threat associated with DRM tools arises from poorly designed tools intended to enforce DRM operations against the (assumed) ill will of the users. In other words, the DRM tools must thwart and override user commands. Ideally these commands are limited to those related to copyrighted content (music, video, etc.); but if the DRM tools are not carefully developed their powerful over-ride capabilities might be turned to unintended purposes, which would threaten the assurance of not only the device upon which they reside plus all other assets on the network, plus the network itself.

This threat related to poorly developed DRM software was first seen in November of 2005, when DRM software distributed by Sony Music created a vulnerability on user PCs, which was exploited by a virus to completely compromise any system upon which the DRM software was installed. The Sony DRM software, developed to override user commands and prevent copying, installed a "root kit" on the user machine. A "root kit" is a software tool that allows an application or user to have complete control over the most basic functioning of a system using relatively simple commands. Normally, installation of such a tool could not occur without the user agreeing to the installation at several points along the way. Because the users knew the software installation was related to Sony DRM, they allowed the installation of the DRM software that contained an unadvertised root kit. The root kit was required in order for the DRM software to prevent copyright violations in a manner that did not give the user any options to prevent the override. The primary flaw with this Sony Music DRM tool was that once the root kit was installed, any other application could employ it too. Given that DRM tools must a) face the most severe threat agents, b) override user commands on powerful and complex devices (PCs) and, eventually, c) manage financial transactions associated with DRM, there will be many more DRM vulnerabilities in the future.

In the wider area of Transparent convergence, tools for attacking converged assets are readily available and, in fact, are not in any way specialized; they are well known testing/hacking tools just turned against the poorly implemented stacks of SCADA, Physical Security, Transaction or Metering systems. The British Columbia Institute of Technology (BCIT) and Eric Byres have demonstrated catastrophic attacks against SCADA Programmable Logic Controls (PLCs), the workhorse of SCADA systems, using the IP Stack Integirty Checker (ISIC)[40] to generate large numbers of malformed ethernet, TCP/UDP/IP and ICMP packets. This tool tests for fundamental issues around the stability of the device on the network. The PLCs tested do not even have the basics right! This is merely one example of converged assets undergoing trial-by-fire on IP networks, re-learning the hard lessons of the past.

Of particular concern within the area of transparent convergence are SCADA systems and the fact that most firewalls are not aware of SCADA protocols.[41] In order for PLCs to have access to

---

[40] http://www.packetfactory.net/Projects/ISIC.
[41] NISCC Good Practice Guide on Firewall Deployment for SCADA and Process Control Networks, National Infrastructure Security Co-ordination Centre, UK Government, Feb 2005, pg 3.

the centralized components that manage the SCADA telemetry (the Data Historian) from the industrial/manufacturing WAN, or from the Data Historian to the industrial WAN and the PCL, general service ports will have to be implemented, which means that any protocol can traverse the network boundaries through these ports. At this time, none of the commercially available firewall products support protocol filtering on any SCADA protocols.

Overall, Transparent convergence offers some of the most serious challenges to the assurance of converged IP networks. A wide range of manufacturing and control protocols have simply been ported without security rigor to an IP carrier and will remain in wide use for a long time to come. For example, oil and gas are known to use MODBUS protocol and power utilities are known to prefer DNP3 as a SCADA protocol. These protocols are not built for the level of hostility or threat present on IP networks and especially the Internet. The MODBUS protocol was analyzed for security features and was found to have:

- No capacity to support confidentiality; all messages are clear text
- No integrity checks
- No authentication checks
- Simplistic framing (i.e., no tracking of which frames should follow which), allowing packet injection with no obstacles[42]

Vast investments have been made in SCADA equipment that cannot be easily upgraded to more secure versions of the control protocols. In many cases these devices simply can not be upgraded to IP. A way to deal with legacy equipment is to place some sort of communication conversion device between the legacy device and the modern IP/ethernet network. SCADA systems and video cameras for physical security and intercom systems are examples, using Analog to Digital Converters (ADCs) and Digital to Analog Converters (DACs). Because the number of such legacy devices is so high, the conversion component market is characterized by small players selling many devices at low margins. These devices have been designed for sustaining baseline functionality after migration to a modern IP network, not security.

---

[42] The Use of Attack Trees in Assessing Vulnerabilities in Scada Systems, Eric Bryes, BC Institute of Technology, 2005.

The upshot of this information is that any low sophistication, low resource threat agent that can logically "see" a SCADA device through any other connected IP network can wreak havoc.

Concerning poor network architecture of otherwise robust protocols, real-time applications like VOIP, entertainment and media, and physical security (video monitoring) use UDP, which does not involve the signaling overhead of TCP and is therefore faster. This also means that these assets will not detect or respond to degrading QoS issues by slowing down the data flows. These protocol architectures can result in UDP-based applications clashing and disrupting TCP applications.[43] Without careful planning and testing, real-time applications based upon UDP could simply hog the network and slow TCP-based assets to a crawl: email slows, financial transactions are delayed. Concurrently, the real-time applications have entered a war of attrition on the network, consuming bandwidth to the point where users stop using.

Poor architectural planning and provisioning also come into play as converged assets enter the IP network and utilize network-based services such as DHCP services and directory services to support address allocation and user authentication, look-up, and accounting, respectively. Such network-based services become a single point of failure and can have significant impact on the assurance of the converged assets. These service will often require new architectures to accommodate increased criticality associated with their pivotal roles in supporting converged assets. For instance, all Triple Play services will revolve around not just the specific asset's infrastructure, but also DHCP and Directory services as a minimum. Managers who have come to take the robustness and capacity of these services for granted may face rude awakenings as converged applications start to increase loads not only on the network-based services themselves, but the network segments that connect these services to the organization as a whole.

---

[43] Providing End-to-End QoS for IP-based Latency-sensitive Applications, Dissertation Proposal, Chen-Nee Chuah, University of California at Berkely, 2002 pg14.

Green Protocols, Stacks, and Architectures

Asset	Agent/Event		Threat Assessment					Risk Assessment	
		Class of Threat	Likelihood	Consequences of Occurrence	Impact	Exposure Rating	Existing Safeguards	Vulnerabilities	Risk
Data	• Protocol design flaws • Protocol implementation flaws legacy Architectures meet converged assets	Confidentiality Integrity Availability	High	Denial of service, compromise of systems and infrastructure	Grave	9	Automated vendor-patch install on desktops, patching services, altering services, IDS/IPS	Unauthorized access to systems and release of personal data equals regulatory breach, system outage and lost productivity, UDP-based service	Low
VOIP	• DRM tools • Unpatched systems • Stack-vendor vulnerabilities • Testing tools become hacking tools • Weak legacy protocols Poor architecture	Confidentiality Integrity Availability	High	Lost intellectual property, lost productivity, infrastructure compromise	Grave	9	Vendors patches, VLAN best practice	Call intercept[44], VOIP SPIT[45] and Phishing[46]; unauthorized access to systems and release of personal data equals regulatory breach, system outage and lost productivity, UDP-based service	High

Entertainment and Media	• Poor architecture	Confidentiality Integrity Availability	High	Loss of TV service, unauthorized access to services, infrastructure and system compromise	Grave	9	Vendors patches, VLAN best practice	Unauthorized access to systems and release of personal data, regulatory breach, system outage and lost productivity, UDP-based service	High
Physical		Confidentiality Integrity Availability	High	Delay in access to sites, loss of video surveillance, system compromise, infrastructure compromise	Grave	9	Vendors patches	UDP-based service, employee productivity, physical breaches undetected or suspected	High
SCADA		Confidentiality Integrity Availability	High	Loss of control of manufacturing processes, infrastructure compromise	Grave	9	Vendors patches, isolated ethernet as best practice	Unauthorized access to systems and release of production data, system outage and lost productivity	High
Banking		Confidentiality Integrity Availability	High	Transactions unable to execute, infrastructure compromise	Grave	9	Dedicated networks, VPN and public-key authentication	System outage and lost transaction equals regulatory breach	Medium

(Continued)

Green Protocols, Stacks, and Architectures (Continued)

Asset	Agent/Event	Class of Threat	Likelihood	Consequences of Occurrence	Impact	Exposure Rating	Existing Safeguards	Vulnerabilities	Risk
		Threat Assessment						**Risk Assessment**	
Facilities		Confidentiality Integrity Availability	High	Loss of control of lighting, heating, cooling, infrastructure compromise	Grave	9	Vendor patches, VLAN as best practice	Unauthorized access to systems and release of production data, system outage and lost productivity	High
Metering		Confidentiality Integrity Availability	High	Loss of remote control of devices, falsification of data, infrastructure compromise	Grave	9	Vendor patches, isolated ethernet as best practice	Unauthorized access to systems and release of production data, system outage and lost productivity	High

[44]VoIP Vulnerabilities: Registration Hijacking, http://www.voip-magazine.com/content/view/108/52/

[45]Spam of Internet Telephony (SPIT), Rosie Lombardi, IT World Canada, June 24, 2005.

[46]email to VOIPSA Technical Working Group, April 13, 2005.

End Point Security

An end-point is the most remote part of the network, the device in the field, or the desktop computer. The end point may be the VOIP phone or the PLC on the factory floor. End-points are usually the "client" in client–server relationships and are often dedicated to a single user. As more and more assets converge on the IP network, there will be more and more end-points of increasingly different technical capabilities and profiles. Some will be highly powerful and complex systems (like desktops), and some will be very simple, dedicated devices like CCTV cameras, smoke detectors, or thermostats. The security requirements and capabilities of these devices will vary greatly, but the crux of this matter is that the assurance requirements of an asset is not commensurate with the device's ability to deal with threats. This is the case with virtually all converged devices that are not part of the "old school" data network (devices used to access the Internet environment) (Fig. 1).

Network security architecture typically contains a firewall at the network interfaces between the internal network and the external network (the Internet or third-party network). This approach has served

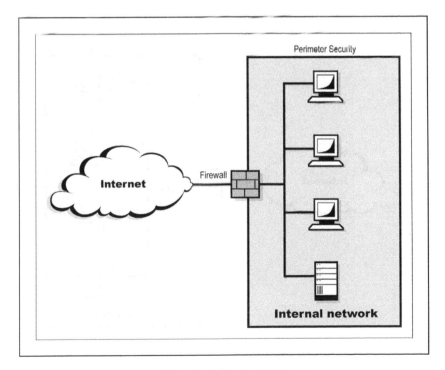

Figure 1 Perimeter security.

well for the last decade but it has clearly reached its limits with converged networks that support potentially dozens of different corporate assets and, more importantly, the entire information communications and technology capabilities of the organization. Perimeter models are fundamentally flawed because once a threat makes it past the hardened perimeter, it can run amok within the network. The contemporary approach to security for end-point devices is to secure the perimeter of the network first, then attempt to deploy secondary security on the network and tertiary security at the end-points as a back-up and last line of defense. This is also referred to as a logical form of "defense in depth" (Fig. 2). Defense in depth attempts to address this issue by applying multiple layers to security which starts at the perimeter that extends throughout the networks down to the end-point. Unfortunately, defense in depth is a mother-hood statement and guidance; it is not an architecture, methodology, application, or process. In the Chapter 4 we will discuss some defense in depth controls and safeguards relative to end-point security.

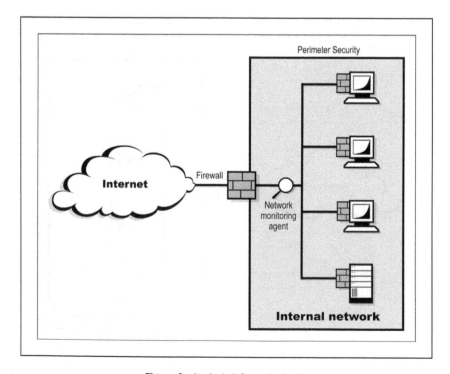

Figure 2 Logical defense in depth.

New security paradigms are currently being promoted as a means to address the flaws of perimeter security. Different equipment vendors have different names for what amounts to proposed improvement in security capability by increased monitoring of the internal network. According to the component vendors, new components are introduced to the core network to monitor threats (which can be defined in different ways) and react to threats with varying degrees of semi-automated quarantine or disabling of network devices. For instance, a computer that is plugged into a network that has a virus would be automatically isolated by the network management equipment, and an alert sent to the administrator. The challenge for the network decision makers concerning this new security paradigm is understanding to what extent converged applications, other than data applications, benefit and are supported.

End-point security for remote devices under Transparent convergence (such as SCADA and CCTV/monitoring) will become very important since they are the sources of the data. But many of these devices are built on proprietary systems with minimum, single-purpose operating systems not compatible with commercially available end-point security products like host-based firewalls, anti-virus or even logical access controls. In Transparent convergence "...there are a number reasons that standard IT security standards can't be directly applied [due to]...the nature of process control systems, with their reliance on unusual operating systems and applications, means that many of the software-based security solutions will not run, or if they do run, they will interfere with the process systems."[47] These facts make defense in depth a challenge to implement within converged ICT networks in the medium term.

The fact that implementing host-based security is out of the question for many end-points forces the stakes for perimeter and network-hygiene related technologies even higher. This is especially true when network managers are dealing with hundreds of thousands of end-point devices. End-point devises increasingly represent the critical components in the network, as opposed to the centralized services and databases that we traditionally think of as the soft, chewy middle that we need to protect. Convergence will drive value and vulnerability out to the end points.

---

[47] Worlds in Collision - Ethernet and the Factory Floor, Eric Byres, BCIT, 2005.

End Point Security

Asset	Threat Assessment						Risk Assessment		
	Agent/Event	Class of Threat	Likelihood	Consequences of Occurrence	Impact	Exposure Rating	Existing Safeguards	Vulnerabilities	Risk
Data	• Malicious insider • Hacker • Virus or worm	Confidentiality Integrity Availability	High	Compromise of systems and infrastructure	Grave	9	Host firewalls, anti-virus, IDS services, patch management tools, vulnerability reporting services, device authentication services, session security (SSL/VPN)	Unpatched systems, poor administration, user error	Low
VOIP		Confidentiality Integrity Availability	High	Lost intellectual property, lost productivity, infrastructure compromise	Grave	9	SIP and H.323 Proxy servers, WAN/LAN/VLAN firewall, manually applied vendors patches	Attack from localized source (inside the LAN), external VOIP SPIT, denial of service	High

Entertainment and Media	Confidentiality Integrity Availability	High	Loss of TV service, Unauthorized access to services infrastructure compromise	Grave	9	Proxy servers on General Service Ports WAN/LAN/VLAN firewall, manually applied vendor patches	Attack from localized source (inside the LAN), externally-based denial of service	High
Physical	Confidentiality Integrity Availability	High	Delay of access to sites, loss of video surveillance, system, compromise, infrastructure compromise	Grave	9	Proxy servers on General Service Ports, WAN/LAN/VLAN firewall, manually applied vendor patches	Attack froml ocalized source (inside the LAN)	High
SCADA	Confidentiality Integrity Availability	High	Loss of control of manufacturing processes, infrastructure compromise	Grave	9	Proxy servers on General Service Ports, WAN/LAN/VLAN firewall, manually applied vendor patches	Attack from localized source (inside the LAN)	High

(Continued)

End Point Security (Continued)

Asset	Threat Assessment						Risk Assessment		
	Agent/Event	Class of Threat	Likelihood	Consequences of Occurrence	Impact	Exposure Rating	Existing Safeguards	Vulnerabilities	Risk
Banking		Confidentiality Integrity Availability	High	Transactions unable to execute, infrastructure compromise	Grave	9	Manually applied patch management tools, vulnerability reporting services, device authentication services, session security (SSL/VPN)	Attack from localized source (inside the LAN)	Low
Facilities		Confidentiality Integrity Availability	High	Loss of control of lighting, heating, cooling, infrastructure compromise	Grave	9	Proxy servers on General Service Ports, WAN/LAN/VLAN firewall, manually applied vendor patches	Attack from localized source (inside the LAN)	High
Metering		Confidentiality Integrity Availability	High	Loss of remote control of devices, falsification of data, infrastructure compromise	Grave	9	Proxy servers on General Service Ports, WAN/LAN/VLAN firewall, manually applied vendor patches	Attack from localized source (inside the LAN)	High

CONCLUSION

The purpose of this chapter was to discuss threats to converged ICT assets that are new and or different from what is the status quo under contemporary, data-only IP networks. This was not an attempt to create a taxonomy of all ICT threats by any means. Specific questions that may remain for readers is: Which of these newly identified classes of threats to converged assets is the most potent? Which require immediate attention? Such a judgment would be purely subjective to the organization asking the question and the value of the distinct converged assets. For instance, telecom suppliers have a much greater interest in the threats presented by Walled Gardens than a hospital.

Figure 5 is a "risk map," drawn from the Enterprise Risk Management school of thinking. The purpose of a risk map is to provide management with easily consumable information about risks and their likelihood and impact. The metrics implemented here are qualitative and are aggregated estimates across all industries.

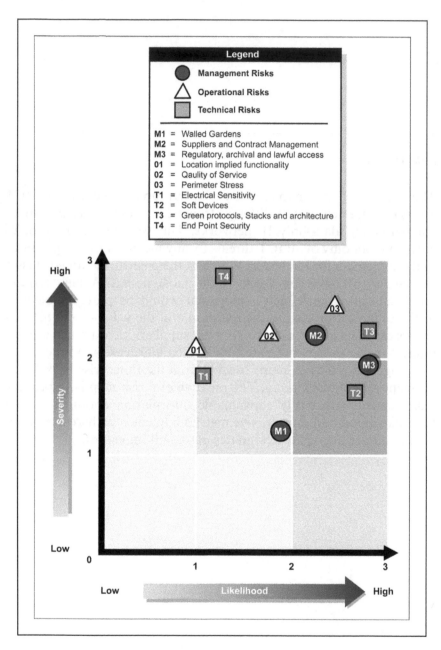

Figure 3 Risk map

4

Controls and Safeguards in the All-IP World

Bell Security Solutions, Inc.

CONTRIBUTING AUTHORS: George McBride
Lucent Technologies
Robert Prudhomme
InCode Wireless

- **INTRODUCTION**
- **TARGET AUDIENCE**
- **DESCRIPTIVE TECHNIQUES: CONTROL AND SAFEGUARD WORKSHEETS**
- **SAMPLE WORKSHEET**
  Assessment Paradigm
- **MANAGEMENT CONTROLS**
- **OPERATIONAL CONTROLS**
  Technical Threats
- **CONCLUSION**

129

INTRODUCTION

"Risk management is the process of assessing risk, taking steps to reduce risk to an acceptable level, and maintaining that level of risk."[1] This chapter extends our risk management exercise into the area of reducing converged ICT risks through proactive controls and safeguards that organizations may employ to improve assurance. This chapter contains suggested controls and safeguards to mitigate or reduce the risks posed from the enumerated threats in Chapter 3. Typically, a good control system will balance prevention, detection, response and recovery safeguards;[2] this chapter uses this framework of prevent/detect/respond/recover to present the safeguards around converged assets. Chapter 5: Managing Assurance, will focus on the broader management techniques associated with the safeguards described here.

Continuing the format of Chapter 3, we will attempt to highlight how controls and safeguards can be extended to mitigate the risks against the body of converged assets: how the effectiveness of a control or safeguard can be leveraged across multiple, converged assets to contain cost and delivery efficiencies in converged ICT security. Finally, this chapter will discuss and focus on controls and safeguards in Tables 1 to 3.

---

[1] NIST 800-26, pg A-5.
[2] Information Systems Audit and Control Association, COBIT Control Objectives, pg 58.

Table 1 Management Control and Safeguard Summary

Control Category	Controls and Safeguards Associated with:			
	Prevent	Detect	Respond	Recover
Management	**Walled Gardens:**			
	Customer centric routing	Internal audit	Digital Rights Management traceability	
	Top-tier supplier MPLs			
	Suppliers and Contract Management:			
	Supplier profile assessment		Supplier hedging and exit clauses	
	Expose hidden costs			
	Disperse infrastructure risks			
	Regulatory, Archival, and Lawful Access Requirements:			
	Regulatory assurance checklist			Regulatory assurance checklist
	Log management			
	Assistance to LEAs policy			
	Encryption policy			
	Roaming transparency			

Table 2 Operational Control and Safeguard Summary

Control Category	Controls and Safeguards Associated With:			
	Prevent	Detect	Respond	Recover
Operational	**Location-Implied Functionality:**			
	Location attribute binding	Scheduled re-		
	Isolation of location	authentication of		
	sensitive devices	devices		
	Control functions of IMS			
	Quality of Service:			
	Patch management	Network	Network	
		monitoring	monitoring	
	Readiness and Testing			
	Environment (RATE)			
	Acceleration of network			
	components			
	MPLS			
	Perimeter Stress:			
	Standardize on two-factor	Telephony firewalls	CIRT	
	authentication	VOIP device		
	User awareness	segregation		
	Change control	Sustained		
	Mandate best practices	monitoring		
	at perimeter			
	Telephony firewalls			
	VOIP device segregation			
	Impact assessment			
	checklists			
	IMS controls			

Table 3 Technical Control and Safeguard Summary

Control Category	Controls and Safeguards Associated With:			
	Prevent	Detect	Respond	Recover
Technical	**Electrical Environment Sensitivity:**			
	PoE	Security event		
	Central office power	management (SEM)		
	Cable deployment			
	Mandate best practices at perimeter			
	Soft Devices:			
	Limit device connections	SEM	CIRT	
	Internal switching controls	IDS/IPS		
	Session security			
	End-point security			
	Green Protocols, Stacks, and Architectures:			
	TRAs	SEM	CIRT	CIRT
	Application firewalls	Network monitoring tools		Formalized feedback to
	Hardened and HA DHCP/LDAP	Open source information tools		procurement processes
	Separate logical networks	RATE		
Technical *(Cont.)*	Vendor communications			
	End Point Security:			
End-point security	SEM	CIRT	CIRT	
	Open-source information tools	Static IP addresses		
	Network-based security	Converged device proxies		
		End-point hardening		

TARGET AUDIENCE

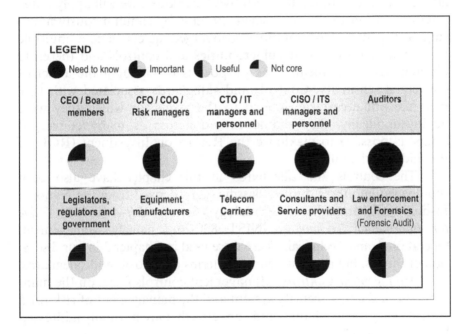

DESCRIPTIVE TECHNIQUES: CONTROL AND SAFEGUARD WORKSHEETS

The concept of risk worksheets will be continued from Chapter 3, with some of the summary information from those worksheets transposed into the control and safeguard worksheets. Controls and safeguards will be described using a standardized tabular format that draws heavily from traditional, formalized Threat Risk Assessment (TRA) processes and worksheets using qualitative metrics. In addition to the traditional descriptive techniques, we will apply a distinct dimension to this assessment process by simultaneously assessing a threat against multiple, converged assets. These multiple assets may have different vulnerabilities and controls and therefore different risk assessments. The purpose is to highlight the affect of converged sensitivity: Controls and safeguards associated with ICT risks are not necessarily limited to the assets for which they were deployed; ideally, they should extend across as many converged assets as possible to maximize the Return on Investment (ROI) of the additional controls.

The controls and safeguards in this chapter have also been sub-divided into three distinct classifications derived from the National Institute of Standards and Technology's *Security Self-Assessment Guide for Information Technology* (NIST 800-26);[3] namely Management, Operational, and Technical. These were used in Chapter 3 in our discussion of threats, but are now defined in terms of controls and safeguards:

Management Controls: Management controls focus on the management of the ICT security system and the management of risk for a system. They are techniques and concerns that are normally addressed by management.[4]

Operational Controls: Operational controls address security methods focusing on mechanisms primarily implemented and executed by people (as opposed to systems). These controls are put in place to improve the security of a particular system (or group of systems) and often require technical or specialized expertise and often rely upon management activities as well as technical controls.[5]

---

[3] NIST 800-26 - http://csrc.nist.gov/publications/nistpubs/800-26/sp800-26.pdf.
[4] NIST 800-26, pg A-5.
[5] NIST 800-26, pg A-18.

Technical Controls: Technical controls focus on security controls that the ICT system executes itself. The controls provide automated protection for unauthorized access or misuse, facilitate detection of security violations, and support security requirements for applications and data.[6]

An additional tool for categorizing the controls and safeguards within this chapter will be employed. Specifically, there are many different methodologies for dealing with network presence but the general consensus is that they all generally come down to four distinct phases:

1. Protect
2. Detect
3. Respond
4. Recover

We will utilize this framework for the discussion of controls and safeguards within the broader control categories, and how they might be implemented to preserve the assurance of the converged network.

---

[6] NIST 800-26, pg A-43.

SAMPLE WORKSHEET

The worksheets in this chapter link the threats described in Chapter 3 with proposed controls and safeguards, and supply an assessment of the residual risk retained after the controls and safeguards have been put into place. See the sample worksheet on the next page.

Assessment Paradigm

The "reasonableness" of the assessment of controls and safeguards is a subjective judgment based upon assurance requirements of a given asset. The assessments provided here are merely intended to be samples drawn against a hypothetical, large, converged organization with requirements for a commercial-grade of assurance for its assets. For our purposes, a commercial grade of assurance is defined as one required to support entity-level risks as discussed in Chapter 2 (see Fig. 3 in chapter 2), but not assurance required for national-security purposes. Therefore the assessment guidance provided in this chapter is not intended to support the entire range of possible assurance requirements. In some cases, too much assurance may be generated (assurance out of proportion to costs/risks), and in other cases it is possible that too little assurance will be generated. Organizations and readers will need to conduct their own internal sensitivity analyses in order to generate proper metrics and assessments around the value of their converged assets and thereby have a foundation upon which to judge the accuracy of these sample assessments, controls, and safeguards.

Threat number	Number assigned to this threat for tracking against threats in Chapter 3				
Discussion	Finite definition of the threat. Discussion of the threat and potential forms that it may take.				
Asset	The specific type of converged asset				
	Recommendations				
	Threat Assessment	Risk Assessment	Proposed Controls and Safeguards	Residual Risks	Assessment of Safeguards
	Threats that may target the described converged asset, either as an agent or an event expressed as a qualitative exposure rating from 1 to 9. (See Chapter 3.)	Risk assessment is an evaluation of the chance of vulnerabilities being exploited, based on the effectiveness of existing or proposed security safeguards.[7] (See Chapter 3.)	RECOMMEND implementation of new safeguards or removal of unnecessary safeguards	ASSESS the projected risk as: • Low • Medium • High	ASSESS the safeguards as: • Completely satisfactory • Satisfactory in most aspects—Assurance will rapidly degrade • Needs improvement—Constant attention required as technology and tools develop

[7] Royal Canadian Mounted Police Threat Risk Assessment Methodology Guide 1994.

MANAGEMENT CONTROLS

Management controls focus on the management of the ICT security system and the management of risk for a system. They are techniques and concerns that are normally addressed by management.[8]

Walled Gardens

In Chapter 3 we discussed the threats, vulnerabilities, and risks associated with Walled Gardens. These risks were largely associated with the Triple Play variant of convergence: Data, Voice, and Video (Entertainment and Media) available through IP. To review briefly, the risks posed by the Walled Garden represent:

- Lack of any QoS management between ISPs
- Lack of any means to associate phone numbers to IP addresses
- The temptation to establish distribution and marketing bottlenecks to the detriment of customers, partners, and suppliers

Addressing the lack of QoS management between ISPs is very problematic, as mentioned in Chapter 3, because the ISPs are fundamentally concerned with internal network efficiency and less so with the traffic leaving their networks. Any given carrier will be driven to sell customers a complete end-to-end network solution, and one of the major selling points is the QoS and other assurance elements that can be made available. [For instance, Multi-Protocol Label Switching (MPLS) can offer both QoS and VPN-type services.] Bear in mind, however, that if the ISP in question does not have services available in all of your organization's points of presence, they cannot provide solutions to QoS issues because they do not control the infrastructure. Furthermore, ISPs do not have any incentives to rationalize the QoS capability of traffic passing between their networks because to do so would further commoditize the provision of network transport services.

Managers can adopt a few different strategies to try and improve QoS between ISPs in order to maximize the returns associated with their investments in converged technologies.

---

[8] NIST 800-26, pg A-5.

Protection: Protection is the implementation of management countermeasures to prevent degradation in services on the converged network. These safeguards may take the following forms on a converged
network:

1. *Customer-Centric Routing.* During the contracting process for
   network services, managers can specify the requirements around
   service levels which include some non-typical provisions such as
   the number of network-hops to the network interchanges with
   other ISPs. (Typical SLAs will already have provisions around
   bandwidth speeds, uptime/availability, error rates, and packet
   loss rates.) This could allow data to take the most direct route
   through the networks and greatly reduce the number of routers
   through which VOIP or delay-sensitive traffic must flow. In
   order to make these sorts of requests, managers will require
   detailed information not only about the topology of the ISPs
   under consideration, but also the topology of the peering ISP
   with which QoS is to be preserved. It may likely be that managers will need to collect and gather network information from
   several ISPs—depending on the number of office locations
   involved.
2. *Top-Tier Suppliers.* If QoS between ISPs is important, it is
   necessary to chose ISPs that have the ability to meet routing
   demands right to the major network interchanges. Small ISPs
   will purchase wholesale bandwidth from large ISPs who provide the core network and usually the peering interchanges. If
   an organization is not dealing with a major ISP that runs
   and manages some of the relatively few major peering and network interchange points, then they cannot affect the necessary
   changes. This fact is also a salient component of Supplier and
   Contract Management. In the end, it will be up to informed
   ICT managers and executive pressure on these managers to
   drive the market in the direction required to support QoS to
   support converged applications. By placing such demands
   within the terms of contracts, managers will drive the market
   in the direction that they need to support QoS requirements
   and break out of the Walled Garden and leveraging convergence to the maximum benefit of their business.
3. *Peering of IP to ENUM Mappings.* The issue of reconciling static
   phone numbers with dynamic IP addresses is an insidious risk to
   the assurance of VOIP and does not offer any clear solutions.
   Within the Walled Garden, ISPs and especially organizations

can map phone numbers to IP addresses through a variety of directory-based systems with a significant degree of assurance, because they control the allocation of IP addresses and the security of the network components that support the mappings, such as directory servers. Once outside the Walled Garden, users of VOIP must essentially rely upon the PSTN to deliver calls with any degree of assurance because there is not yet any way to manage phone-number-to-IP address mapping securely, as discussed in Chapter 3. Whether deploying within a single office building or to organizations around the world, managers need to document at which point assets such as VOIP will interact outside the Walled Garden and how this might impact services.

For managers, the short-term solution to phone-number-to-IP-address-mapping is related to the QoS solutions (use brute force—throw bandwidth at it), coupled with old VPN technologies or possibly new VPN technologies based upon MPLS.[9] If the issue of QoS between peering ISPs can be addressed, then VPNs can be installed between sites and intra- or inter-organizational links can be established for VOIP traffic. Each organization could refer to the others phone-number-to-IP address directory internally and thereby by-pass the PSTN between them. For large organizations with large communication volumes among a few suppliers, customers, and partners this could result in significant savings. Establishing these sorts of agreements is itself a significant security operation but is well within the bounds of known practice.

Detection: Managing contracts and fulfillment on an on-going basis. These safeguards may take the following forms on a converged network:

4. *Internal Auditing*. Managing the assurance of converged networks will entail the development and implementation of mutually agreed upon safeguards within all connected organizations, and the on-going maintenance of these safeguards through testing and audit processes. These processes would normally be conducted by an internal audit team reporting directly to the CEO or Board.

---

[9] Analysis of MPLS-based IP VPN Security: Comparison to Traditional L2VPNs such as ATM and Frame Relay, and Deployment Guidelines, Cisco Systems, 2004.

This group would have a defined mandate for auditing a wide range of assurance-related elements of the Walled Garden; for example, standards for network interconnectivity, VPN device security, or directory security would have to be established, as would standards and procedures for the operation and management of any devices associated with the VPN services supporting VOIP.

Response: Reaction to assurance events within the Walled Garden. These safeguards may take the following forms on a converged network:

5.   An Internal Audit is again a useful control and safeguard for the Walled Garden because the results of audits should contain both recommendations around remediation and a remediation plan. Furthermore, the internal stakeholders should have already had an opportunity to review the audit results and to commence remedial activities.

6.   Digital Rights Management (DRM) is a major issue for Entertainment and Media convergence and one of the few apparent means of enforcement—and therefore paying the creators of the content—is through a Walled Garden. Billing, like phone-number to IP-address mappings, requires knowledge of the destination of content (traceability) in order for it to be billable, even if this knowledge is not related to an IP address but some authentication token which can be traced for billing purposes. While authentication token-devices are available from a variety of manufacturers, authentication tokens that are simple yet provide the assurance upon which to base billions of dollars of content-consumption transactions are not available as commodity items. The provision and management of authentication tokens is an adjunct to a Walled Garden and is greatly facilitated by the existence of a Walled Garden because of the combination of a controlled network environment (defined IP ranges, defined MAC ranges) with a controlled authentication environment (defined authorities, cryptographic algorithms and specifications). There remains the issue that content producers (artists) may find themselves not particularly benefiting from convergence and the new opportunities for distribution and marketing, but the current crisis around the collection of royalties and theft of intellectual property (copyright infringement) override such concerns.

Recovery Safeguards Around Supplier and Contract Management: No stipulation.

Macaulay, McBride, and Prudhomme

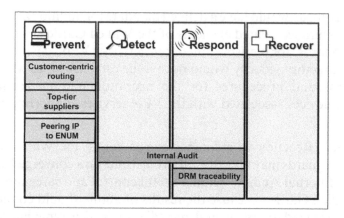

Asset			Recommendations		
	Threat Assessment	Risk Assessment	Proposed Controls and Safeguards	Residual Risks	Assessment of Safeguards
Data	7	Low	NA	NA	Satisfactory in most aspects
VOIP	8	High	• Customer-centric routing • Top-tier suppliers • Peering IP to ENUM • Internal audit	Medium ISPs refuse to adjust or collude Slow development universal of phone-number-to-IP mapping services	Needs improvement
Entertainment and Media	9	High	DMR traceability	High Digital Rights Management overrides "choice issues" currently	Needs improvement
Physical	7	Low	NA	NA	Satisfactory in most aspects
SCADA	7	Low	NA	NA	Satisfactory in most aspects
Banking	7	Low	NA	NA	Satisfactory in most aspects
Facilities	7	Low	NA	NA	Satisfactory in most aspects
Metering	7	Low	NA	NA	Satisfactory in most aspects

Suppliers and Contract Management

The purpose of this section is to highlight supplier and contract controls that may be unique or accentuated under ICT convergence; this section is not intended to be a compilation of all likely safeguards and controls around supplier and contract management.

Protection: The implementation of management countermeasures to prevent degradation in services on the converged network. These safeguards may take the following forms on a converged network:

1. *Supplier Profile Assessment.* It would be too much to expect that senior management become involved in granular operational issues like supplier and contract management; however, senior management needs to approve the requirements and selection criteria to provide guidance around which particular conditions (risks) are to be observed when selecting vendors or agreeing to contract conditions. Selection criteria for suppliers should never be ad hoc:

   - Supplier selection should be a managed processes with defined and documented criteria, approved by senior management and applied by contract or middle managers.
   - Supplier stability should be a crucial element of the vendor's selection process. Vendors should possess characteristics that provide a reasonable amount of assurance that they will remain in business for at least the duration of the contract, or the expected useful life of the equipment being provided. In the age of de-regulated and newly developing convergence technologies, this is not a given.
   - Consider to what degree ICT convergence is acknowledged in their product roadmap and documentation. Is the supplier aware of the requirement for assurance of newly converged assets and are the products being testing in this environment? There are a wide variety of factors that may be used to judge the potential business viability of a vendor, but these factors should be viewed from the perspective of a changing/converging ICT environment. For example, is the vendor aware of convergence and is clearly a thought leader in this area? Or is the vendor only release "IP-enabled," taking advantage of

a market opportunity/requirement? A vendor without a eye on the future of their market may be overtaken rapidly by competitors and out of business well before your equipment is at the end of its useful life.

- In considering out-sourcing services, look at the converged business unit as a distinct part—the business as a whole may be in good shape but the business unit is not. This is especially the case in out-sourced IP-based services. Is the supplier truly committed to this business line or could they possibly close it down? Look at who is running the unit: high-powered, incumbent insiders from "the mothership" or mercenaries parachuted in from outside to take the risk and be expendable if the bets don't pay off? Look at the centricity of the business unit relative to the overall corporate direction and public strategy: how much of a climb-down will the Board or top management have to make to back out of the business? Do they really have a serious personal stake?

- Understand who is the final supplier. For many reasons from tax-planning to regulatory fiat to brand management and marketing, the true owner and controller of a supplier may not be obvious. If issues such as redundant and independent supplies of bandwidth, devices or other primary ICT inputs are critical to a business, then managers must be aware of obscure ownership that may invalidate a particular vendor selection. To address these concerns, look for assurances about the status of the ownership in your contract and, in the event that the ownership changes, retain the right to leave the contract on short notice and without penalty.

The summation of these points is that communications with suppliers should be open, proactive, and frequent, particularly in sectors considered to be critical infrastructure.

2. *Expose Hidden Costs.* In order to maintain the assurance of all assets on the network undergoing asset convergence, costs associated with following elements should be considered as a part of the plan concerning the convergence of the asset:

- Additional bandwidth and device (router/hub) upgrades to support more bandwidth. Emerging best-practices around converged networks indicate that whenever possible, implement critical circuit redundancy using two unrelated telecommunications providers.[10]
- Firewall impacts can result in significant additional costs as the loads on the existing firewalls cannot support more IP applications. As a result, new firewalls must be added, old firewalls replaced or upgraded, and the firewall infrastructure as a whole must undergo a re-fit. There are also hidden risks associated with these sorts of undertakings, such as the risk that the newly implemented and configured firewalls introduce vulnerabilities due to administrative mistakes or oversights. Security Event Management systems (SEMs) can track and report these critical events. (SEMs are covered later in this chapter under Technical Controls.)
- Intrusion monitoring impacts are similar to firewall impacts. The growth of network loads and the introduction of new applications will place burdens on intrusion monitoring capabilities in the form of increased log-volumes and especially the tuning and adjustment to new applications. Sudden, unanticipated increases in the demand for intrusion monitoring resources usually results not in immediate application of more resources, but in allowing intrusion alarms to go unattended or to form a backlog as volumes exceed capacity. The direct result is that intrusion monitoring investments are nullified.
- Migration of an asset to a converged network environment is not a standalone decision around a single converged asset; from a ICT security perspective, it involves many decisions that impact the assurance of all ICT assets overall. Fundamentally, the IP network as a whole must be considered and not just the asset being drawn onto IP.

3. *Disperse Infrastructure Risks.* Mixing and matching in-sourcing and out-sourcing is an effective way to improve the assurance of converged ICT assets. "In-sourcing" refers to the practice of

---

[10] SQL Slammer Worm Lessons Learned for Consideration by the Electricity Sector, North American Electricity Reliability Council, June 20, 2003.

managing assets with full-time employees or contract staff; "out-sourcing" is the opposite: contracting the on-going management of an asset to a third-party entity, which is responsible for staffing and possibly even owns the infrastructure that underpins the asset. In-sourcing and out-sourcing are these days unrelated to the physical location of the asset—customer premises or supplier premises.

Supplier and contract management is not simply about the procurement of equipment and commodity services such as bandwidth; it can also involve the careful choices around what to in-source and what may be out-sourced as a hedge. Hedging between in-sourcing and out-sourcing in the world of converged ICT assets is worth considering because it partially addresses some of the threats associated with having all critical communications systems riding over IP. Hedging through out-sourcing is also another way of speaking about transferring risk related to ICT assets from one organization through contracting processes. In otherwords, the out-source supplier, through their service level agreements, assume some of the risks related to the loss of ICT assurance and accept the liability and sanctions that may be embedded into the supplier contract.

As an example of a hedging technique, consider an organization that has converged its data, voice, physical security (CCTV, Access controls), and industrial controls (SCADA). In this instance, the network is clearly a piece of critical infrastructure whose assurance is paramount. But maintaining the assurance of all the assets goes beyond the network, to the operation and management of the central and end-point devices associated with a given asset; i.e., to the people and the facilities which support these assets. If all converged assets are managed in-house, then the network is merely the most obvious single point of failure impacting all assets. A labor strike or a sick employee who changed a password without telling anyone could bring all communications and business to a halt. This same organization might consider out-sourcing certain converged applications in order to hedge against failures not related to the network. For instance, managed IP Telephony is an option for the organization in this example; while a labor action may make maintaining production capacity difficult, at least customers/suppliers/partners will be able to phone-in and managers will have functional telephony to try to coordinate remediation around the other converged assets that remain managed in-house.

Detection Safeguards Around Supplier and Contract Management: No stipulation.

Response: Safeguards arising from supplier and contract management response issues. These safeguards may take the following forms on a converged network:

4. *Supplier Alternatives and Exit Clauses.* As a matter of due diligence, managers should remain in contact on an annual basis at minimum with competing service providers, if they are not already pro-actively in touch as a matter of sales! Keep abreast of changes in pricing, service levels, and product offerings in the event that a rapid decision must be made concerning a supplier. Have the necessary facts and figures at hand or at least have the necessary contact information available.

   Concerning the current contract, insert specific clauses that not only allow for rapid de-campment from a supplier if they fail to supply negotiated service levels, but also stipulate that the migration must be reasonably facilitated. Some suggested facilitation service measures may be:

   - Availability of technical personnel during non-business hours
   - Rapid execution of change control requests around critical service configurations like DNS records or routing changes
   - Assumption by the supplier of equipment lease obligations which might have been entered into as a matter of the supporting a supplier interface

Recovery Safeguards Around Supplier and Contract Management Risks: No stipulation.

   Prevent and respond are the two elements around which Supplier and Contract Management safeguards can be planned. The safeguards which have been recommended are presented below.

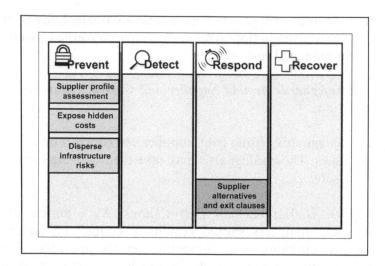

Asset			Recommendations		
	Threat Assess-ment	Risk Assess-ment	Proposed Controls and Safeguards	Residual Risks	Assessment of Safeguards
Data	N/A	N/A	• Defined and management approved selection criteria • Investigation of hidden costs associated with convergence • Hedge using out-sourcing • Supplier alternatives and exit clauses	Low • Other assets converge an impact data assurance	Completely satisfactory
VOIP	8	High		Low	Completely satisfactory
IPTV	9	High		Medium • Available only through third parties, not all safeguards apply	Satisfactory in most aspects
Physical	8	High		Low	Completely satisfactory
SCADA	8	Medium		Low	Completely satisfactory
Banking	7	Low		Low	Completely satisfactory
Facilities	8	Medium		Low	Completely satisfactory
Metering	8	High		Low	Completely satisfactory

Regulatory, Archival and Lawful Access Requirements

Many managers may not fully understand the current regulatory requirements around conventional Data IP networks and applications; fewer still have any inkling of the regulatory requirements as multiple ICT assets converge on IP networks. This is not to say that people are entirely uneducated in these matters; it is a case of the regulatory implications being often vague and unproven.

Protection: Safeguards around regulatory risks.

1. *Regulatory Assurance Checklists.* The best way to start developing controls and safeguards against potential regulatory vulnerabilities is to determine and document the requirements. Consider issues such as retention, disclosure, use, consent, archives, lawful access, and adjust the capabilities that are currently supported and available internally for compliance purposes. Such a document will represent an *Regulatory Assurance Checklists (RAC)* for the organization as a whole. The initial drafts of such documents would be developed through the collaboration of legal, management, and technical team members. The legal members contribute to an understanding of the statutes and regulations, while the management and technical teams communicate the mapping between a legal requirement and tentative safeguards.

    An RAC does not need to be a complex document; simple is better. Ideally, the RAC will start with a simple outline of the statutes and regulations applicable to the organization, and then spell out in simple but clear terms the legal requirements. These requirements should first be related to different converged asset categories (data, voice, physical security), but then specific assets at lower levels as required. From these legal requirements, safeguards should be mapped in a matrix on a one-to-many (legal to safeguard) basis so that no legal requirement is overlooked, with safeguards being grouped as management, operational, or technical. For instance, it is possible that requirements for several safeguards will be generated by a single legal requirement; however, it is also likely that many safeguards will be common across all multiple requirements. See Chapter 5: Managing Assurance for a detailed discussion of RACs.

    Make sure the RAC is propagated to stakeholders and those responsible for day-to-day implementation. In addition, training and awareness around new management policies for both users and administrators is the staple of all good ICT security practices; in the case of regulatory requirements, it is especially important because of the multi-dimensional aspect of legal requirements under converged IP networks. There are many forms of training and awareness that can be implemented, but recommendations about appropriate strategies in this regard are beyond the scope of this book.

As with all policy and strategy undertakings, the biggest threat is that no one is made accountable for the implementation, ongoing support and evergreening of the resulting programs. For this reason it is imperative that documents such as the RAC get executive sponsorship.

2. *Support Privacy.* ICT administration policies should acknowledge that the configuration and usage patterns of converged assets have the potential to reveal a significant amount of detail about an individual and that such information could violate privacy legislation and is clearly against corporate policy. The policy may require ICT administrators and personnel to sign a code of ethics around the management of ICT data. Similarly, configuration and usage patterns of converged assets have the potential to reveal proprietary production or other competitive information and could represent highly sensitive commercial data.

3. *Log-Management Guidance.* Specific log-management policies and procedures need to be established around devices that manage more than one converged asset; such as firewalls, gateways/proxies, IDSs or IPS systems and any other devices that log events of converged assets in one way or another. These policies should stipulate the requirements around:

- Confidentiality requirements of the logged information and access to this information
- Availability and preservation requirements
- Integrity requirements

Each policy should stipulate that procedures be developed, documented, and tested and the status reported to management.

4. *Assistance to Law Enforcement Policies.* These are clearly defined policies to provide guidance to corporate security staff as to what lawful access may mean to them and what the organization is prepared to do to proactively support law enforcement. Conversely, management, administrators, and security staff should know the limits of what they are required to do for law enforcement on an unpaid versus paid basis. This can be a very critical distinction in the event of major litigation against even distant business relations, and could prove to be ruinously costly if undertaken with the assumption that someone somewhere will pay for all the lawful access requests. Make no assumptions about who bears the costs of lawful access; do not assume it is anyone but you!

5. *Encryption Policies Regarding Storage and Management of Personal Data.* Encryption is potentially a very useful tool for regulatory compliance purposes because it can result in some forbearance. For instance, California Law SB 1386 requires that notification be made to any individual whose personal information may have been exposed without authorization (i.e., hacked).[11] The use of encryption to protect data is a recognized safeguard.

6. *Roaming Transparency Is Clearly Highlighted with Service Agreements.* Users are educated to the fact that, as their mobile devices roam from network to network, their account information may be shared for billing and accounting purposes. This is a counter-point to Walled Gardens—the more freedom a user has to procure services, the more privacy risks they may face.

Detection Safeguards Around Regulatory, Archival and Lawful Access Risks:

7. *Audit the Regulatory Assurance Checklist.* Place the RAC within the mandate of the internal audit group and formally audit on an annual basis. Ideally, segment the RAC, and audit portions each quarter.

---

[11] http://www.enterprisestorageforum.com/continuity/features/article.php/3498006

Response: Safeguards arising from regulatory, archival and lawful risks.

8. *IP Multi-Media Subsystem (IMS)*. According to whitepapers on the subject from manufacturers such as Ericsson,[12] the next version IMS will provide lawful access functions that will allow organizations to respond to access requests in standardized fashioned, as defined and implemented by equipment manufacturers. IMS also provides authorization, authentication, and accounting standards, which can act as safeguards against privacy incidents.

Recovery Safeguards Around Supplier and Contract Management Risks:

9. *Regulatory Assurance Checklist*. The RAC will prove a valuable forensic tool during the recovery from regulatory infractions. The RAC should provide an immediate tool to identify where the preventive safeguards failed, what other assets might have been impacted, and who was accountable for the failure. The fact that the RAC can also be employed in the course of recovery will re-enforce the business cases for its development.

Prevent, detect, respond, and recovery are the elements around which recovery, archival, and lawful access safeguards can be planned. The safeguards which have been recommended are presented below.

---

[12] Ericsson, IMS - IP Multi-media Subsystem Whitepaper: the value of using the IMS architecture, October 2004 pg 16

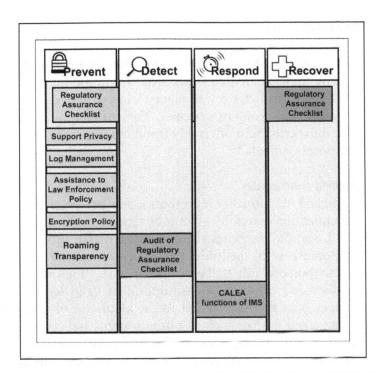

Asset	Threat Assessment	Risk Assessment	Proposed Controls and Safeguards	Residual Risks	Assessment of Safeguards
Data	9	Medium	• Regulatory assurance strategy • Accountability for implementation of strategy • Training and awareness	High • New technologies coupled with new legal requirements result in confusion and mistakes • Management recognizes problem but implements ad hoc solutions specific to individual assets and unconverged ("old fashioned") networks	Needs improvement
VOIP	9	High			
IPTV	8	Medium			
Physical	9	High			
SCADA	6	Low			
Banking	9	High			
Facilities	6	Low			
Metering	9	High			

OPERATIONAL CONTROLS

Operational controls address security methods focusing on mechanisms primarily implemented and executed by people (as opposed to systems). These controls are put in place to improve the security of a particular system (or group of systems). They often require technical or specialized expertise and often rely upon management activities as well as technical controls.[13]

Location-Implied Functionality

Location-implied functionality represents a new perspective on multifactor authentication driven by assurance requirements on converged networks. "Location" becomes the device/hardware equivalent of a biometric because it is the only physically unique property that machines can possess, not to be confused with "logically" unique attributes discussed below. The assumption of valid location attributes will emerge as a critical threat to the assurance of information of many converged devices such as phones, industrial controls, physical security, and metering devices. The end-point security of these devices as a whole will be discussed later, but the location attribute of converged devices is itself a unique attribute, which will require distinct safeguards and controls.

Traditionally, authentication of devices and people has been discussed in terms of three available "factors" or types: 1) what you know—such as a password, 2) what you have—such as a swipe card or USB key, and 3) what you are—a biometric piece of identification like a finger print. All authentication systems will utilize one variety of one of these factors, most typically "what you know" or a password. The more factors employed in the identification of individuals or devices, the more secure the authentication is considered to be. However, in the device-world, the third factor-type "what you are" is not applicable. Machines cannot produce biometrics because they do not contain random elements; they do not possess naturally occurring, random sequences like iris patterns or palm prints that can be used to generate biometrics. But the physical location of many devices is unique and in fact is a critical component in determining if the device in question is both authentic and authorized.

---

[13] NIST 800-26, pg A-18.

It may be argued that devices can be embedded with crypto-graphic capabilities and synchronized random number generators that might simulate a biometric, but this objection has several flaws:

1. What one machine can do, another machine can also do, given the right inputs – but one person can never, ever simulate another person's biometrics.
2. Any unique piece of data embedded or generated by a device is not actually considered a form of biometric because it represents "a) what you know" or "b) what you have", not "c) what you are."
3. Any unique property embedded into a device could, in theory, have been duplicated beforehand, and then embedded in another device.

Prevention Safeguards Around Location-Implied Functionality Risks:

1. *Location-Attribute Binding.* The solution to threats associated with location-implied functionality is to define a form of location-attribute binding and authentication. This means that the device extracts a piece of information (an attribute) from its environment and uses this information in the generation of authentication information, which may be utilized in authentication exchanges such as those under IPSec or those proposed for IP Multi-Media Subsystem (IMS)[14]—the proposed future of real-time applications on IP networks. This location attribute would be considered a consistent value as long as the device remains in the same physical location, but would change if the device moves and would result in either a failure to authenticate or trigger a location-update activity with whatever centralized system is monitoring or concerned with location.

   ▪ *GPS Binding.* For instance, a well-head pump may incorporate a GPS location in the salt values used to generate crypto-graphic keys for authentication. If this GPS value changes the keys change and authentication fails, triggering some sort of remediation.

---

[14] Graham Finnie, Heavy Reading, *IMS and the Future of Network Convergence*, July 2005.

- *RFID Binding.* Another potential means to authenticate location without relying on GPS may be to gather information from other devices in the same proximity, information from RFID tags on nearby equipment for instance. The strength of this approach is that RFID would authenticate using local devices without using the local network—it would be operating out-of-band using short-range radio communications and not the shared, fixed line network.
- *MAC Binding.* A further example may be to link authentication values for devices to highly localized network information such as the Medium Access Control (MAC) address of the layer-2 switches (routers) or other proximate devices (like other end-point devices). This information is generally only available on the local network and cannot be easily determined from external network points. If an attempt was made to send forged device authentication information from an unauthorized network location, the layer-2 MAC information used to generate the authentication information would not match and authentication might fail.
- *IP Binding.* Authentication of end-point devices that possess location-implied requirements but cannot support the safeguards discussed above may attempt to compensate with alternative authentication technologies. Such authentication can take many forms and would likely rely on a single factor of authentication, such as a cryptographic key loaded to the device at manufacture. While this type of authentication would not provide a complete safeguard against the device being accidentally or maliciously moved from its expected location, it would provide an effective safeguard against the generation of forged information, for instance from a laptop connected to the network or even remotely generated illicit packets that get routed to an unauthorized destination. Additionally, if this authentication was paired with a second known piece of information such as the current IP address, then further assurance could be provided around the device's approximate location.

2. *Isolation of Location Sensitive Devices.* The assurance of location implied functionally can be enhanced with more standard technologies and techniques. Any deployment of converged devices

such as VOIP, SCADA, Physical Security, Metering, etc., must ensure that network egress and ingress rules have been applied that limit as far as possible the sources and destinations of data from converged assets. Specifically, configure perimeter firewalls to deny any outbound data from these sources since they have no reason to go outside the network or originate from outside the network. Similarly, configure internal firewalls, routers, and switches to only allow traffic to be routed to and from legitimate internal destinations.

Figure 1 illustrates the type of separation of location-sensitive devices that might be implemented using conventional network architecture techniques. The rule set indicated is for demonstrative purposes only and is not intended to represent the correct expressive syntax for firewall rules.

Figure 1 shows a simplistic network architecture with the isolation of location-sensitive SCADA devices. In this architecture, all traffic passes through a firewall. Information from the industrial network is allowed out but no information is permitted into this network. Users requiring access from the SCADA devices are required to go to a central historian device that will allow inbound connections from the office network. No traffic between the office network and the SCADA network is allowed, even though that is where the operators reside.

3. *IP Multi-Media Subsystem (IMS)*. According to whitepapers on the subject from manufacturers such as Ericsson,[15] the next version of IMS will provide location-authentication features and functions. A potential safeguard available to organizations will be to transition to the evolving version of IMS once available. In the meantime, the other safeguards mentioned in this section are contemporary solutions.

---

[15] Ericsson, IMS – IP Multi-media Subsystem Whitepaper: the value of using the IMS architecture, October 2004 pg 16.

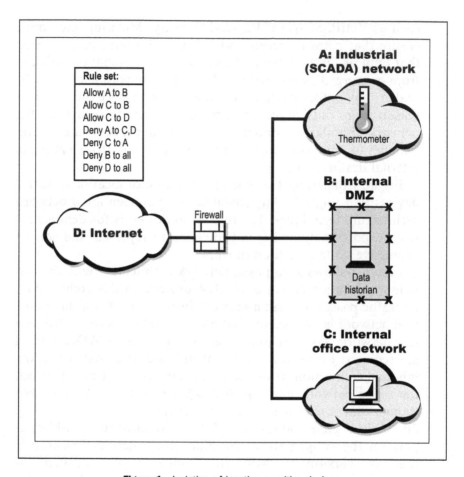

Figure 1   Isolation of location-sensitive devices.

Detection Safeguards Around Location Implied Functionality Risks:

4. *Scheduled Re-authentication.* Because safeguard 1) involves the generation of authentication information using location-attributes values, movement of the device will result in a failure to authenticate; however, this in turn requires that the device is forced to authenticate its location-attribute on a regular basis. This type of functionality is not currently mandated within any converged protocols but does have the potential to be employed in certain evolving protocols.
5. *IMS controls.* IMS implementations will require authentication and re-authentication for converged assets/applications that have been configured with this requirement at the IMS control layer which "comprises network control servers for managing call or session setup, modification and release. ... This layer contains a full suite of support functions, such as provisioning, charging and operations and maintenance."[16]

Response Safeguards Around Location-Implied Functionality Risks: No stipulation.

Recovery Safeguards Around Location-Implied Functionality Risks: No stipulation.

Prevent and respond are the two elements around which location-implied functionality safeguards can be planned. The safeguards which have been recommended are presented below.

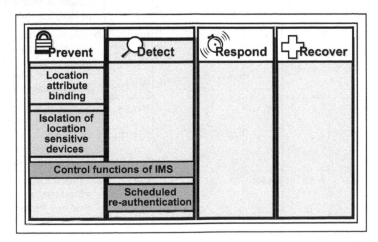

---

[16] Ericsson, IMS – IP Multi-media Subsystem Whitepaper: the value of using the IMS architecture, October 2004 pg 9.

Location-Implied Functionality

Asset	Threat Assessment	Risk Assessment	Proposed Controls and Safeguards	Residual Risks	Recommendations — Assessment of Safeguards
Data	NA	NA	• Location-attribute binding • Isolation of location-sensitive devices • IMS • Scheduled re-authentication	NA	No location-implied assurance expectations/ requirements
VOIP	9	High		High	Needs improvement; functions like E911 will remain problematic until geographically-derived device biometrics can be incorporated
Entertainment and Media	NA	NA			No location-implied assurance requirements
Physical	9	High		Medium	Satisfactory in most aspects; unlikely that data will arrive over the open Internet, therefore it can be highly segregated
SCADA	9	Medium		Medium	Satisfactory in most aspects; unlikely that data will arrive over the open Internet, therefore it can be highly segregated
Banking	9	Medium		Low	Completely satisfactory; few location-implied assurance requirements and good end-point and network security already in place
Facilities	9	High		Medium	Satisfactory in most aspects; unlikely that data will arrive over the open Internet, therefore it can be highly segregated
Metering	9	Medium		Low	Satisfactory in most aspects; unlikely that data will arrive over the open Internet, therefore it can be highly segregated

Quality of Service (QoS): Only as Good as the Weakest Link

In the networking world, QoS is often defined in terms of packet loss (the packet was corrupted or never arrived), latency (transmission delay), and jitter (variability of the transmission delay). Probably the most salient and obvious aspect of QoS is simple uptime and availability. As discussed in Chapter 1, downtime for converged networks has amplified impacts on business as a whole, with devastating impacts on the assurance of the converged assets. One of the key criteria of Service Level Agreements (SLAs) that managers must pay attention to is the uptime/ availability of the network pipes that come into the organization from ISPs. It would be a mistake to assume that the negotiation of adequate availability in a supplier SLA will result in the desired network availability, for the simple reason that QoS starts on the organizational network.

There are a wide variety of techniques, tools, vendors, and service providers from around the world willing to offer solutions related to the preservation of internal availability in the face of a growing number of threats. Virtually all of these techniques, tools, vendors, and service providers are focused on IP data applications and not converged applications (hence this book). However, many of the typical safeguards espoused for IP data QoS and availability apply perfectly well to converged IP applications. On the other hand, there are a few operational safeguards that are specifically relevant to converged assets and the preservation of QoS and availability across all network assets.

Turning our attention to issues of QoS related to packet loss, latency, and jitter: these are extremely devious threats to many converged assets because of their disproportionate impact among converged assets. In other words, packet loss, latency, and jitter have severe impacts on many converged assets, but not all converged assets suffer from loss, latency, and jitter to the same degree.

As the table below illustrates, data is likely the most tolerant converged asset when it comes to loss, latency, and jitter, while most of the other converged applications possess heightened sensitivity.

Table 4 Sensitivity to QoS Features

	Loss	Latency	Jitter
Data	Low	Low	Low
VOIP	Moderate	High	High
Entertainment and Media	Moderate	High	High
Physical Security	Moderate	High	High
SCADA	High	Moderate	Moderate
Banking	Moderate	Moderate	Low
Facilities	Low	Low	Low
Metering	Moderate	Moderate	Moderate

VOIP quality degrades rapidly under latency and jitter but can withstand a certain amount of loss before the human ear detects a degradation in quality. Entertainment and Media is similar to VOIP in the sensitivity to loss, latency, and jitter—possibly more so to loss, because the same eye will detect flaws in motion images. Physical security, such as CCTV monitoring and physical access controls, is again like Entertainment and Media, but with an emphasis not just on video quality but on user experience; people will not tolerate swiping access cards repeatedly for very long—they require near instantaneous responses. SCADA systems are most sensitive to lost data, which represent critical product logs and telemetry information. Similarly, metering is a form of SCADA but directed at billing not production controls and therefore lost packets do not posses the same impact, especially if they can be replayed by the devices. Banking and transaction devices are generally well fortified and historically built to withstand terrible network conditions; IP is not a shock to their systems. From a pure availability perspective, it is more a question of the impact that transaction devices will have on other converged assets and less what other (benign) converged assets will do to converged transaction devices. Finally, facilities management devices (unless they are engaged in metering activities) are used for sustained, longer-term monitoring and less frequent adjustment and change; therefore, loss, latency, or jitter impacts assurance of these assets less. Unfortunately, sensitivity is not uniform and balancing these QoS requirements may prove to be one of the most demanding elements of the all-IP world.

Prevention Safeguards Around Quality of Service Risks:

1. *Inter-Asterik Exchange (IAX)*. IAX is an IETF draft and an emerging protocol for VOIP that is NAT friendly, allowing for potentially better integration of VOIP with firewalls,[17] especially for residential applications or small businesses which might not be in a position to deploy special-purposes session border controllers for SIP or H.323. IAX uses a single port (UDP 4569) for signaling and audio, rather than multiple and distinct ports as in the case of both SIP and H.323.[18]

2. *Patch Management*. Consider network availability as a function of QoS. Work closely with converged systems vendors regarding system security and patch management. As discussed under the heading Green Protocols, Software, and Architectures, many of the converged solutions are new and have not undergone years of field trials and brutalization at the hands of the Internet. They will require additional care and feeding and a good relationship with vendors will be critical to achieving this goal.[19]

3. *RATE*. Implement a Readiness and Testing Environment (RATE) within which patches and upgrades can be tested prior to upgrading any converged system.[20] This is not as simple as it sounds. The difference between what is considered good, cautious implementation techniques and what is, in fact, a truly appropriate testing and implementation regime in light of the converged sensitivity may come as a surprise to many managers. See Chapter 5: Managing Assurance for a discussion of application implementation and testing regimes that would be appropriate to converged networks.

4. *Acceleration of Network Components*. A potential control and safeguard around latency and jitter is to simply accelerate the existing security devices through which asset information passes; namely VPNs and firewalls. These safeguards are tried and true, and remain very useful assurance tools under IP convergence. Managers should seek VPN vendors that have the option to employ hardware-based crypto to speed up

---

[17] http://www.cornfed.com/iax.pdf.

[18] http://www.voip-info.org/wiki-IAX.

[19] SQL Slammer Worm Lessons Learned for Consideration by the Electricity Sector, North American Electricity Reliability Council, June 20, 2003.

[20] SQL Slammer Worm Lessons Learned for Consideration by the Electricity Sector, North American Electricity Reliability Council, June 20, 2003.

processing. The acceleration of processing on traditional controls such as VPNs and firewalls will address some of the threats related to latency and loss—latency because the packets will transverse the network boundaries with less processing delay, and loss because the faster the packets can clear boundary processing, the less likely that boundary device buffers will fill and drop packets resulting in loss. An unfortunate downside of this type of safeguard is that cryptographic processors have a tendency to process larger packets ahead of smaller packet, so the small UDP packets employed for voice and video applications are more frequently dropped under load.[21] Specialized cryptographic engines to support voice and video applications and assets may be required.

5. *MPLS*. As we move further and further into the IP world, the notion of disparate and critical QoS requirements and converged sensitivity of assets is, in part, driving the deployment of Multi-Protocol Label Switching (MPLS). MPLS has attained a significant amount of popularity at the core of the carrier networks of late because it manages to couple the determinism, speed, and QoS controls of established switched technologies like Asynchronous Transfer Mode (ATM) and Frame Relay, with the flexibility and robustness of the Internet Protocol world. [As you might expect, MPLS is developed and propagated through the Internet Engineering Task Force (IETF).[22]] Additionally, "[t]he once faster and higher bandwidth ATM switches are being out-performed by Internet backbone routers. Equally important, MPLS offers simpler mechanisms for packet-oriented traffic engineering and multiservice functionality with the added benefit of greater scalability."[23]

While MPLS is not a solution to QoS issues on the LAN, it may be a consideration for large organizations with broadband WANs in place. Alternately, MPLS QoS management capabilities might be an attractive feature to look for in

---

[21] C-N. Chuah, "Providing End-to-End QoS for IP based Latency sensitive Applications." Technical Report, Dept. of Electrical Engineering and Computer Science, University of California at Berkeley, 2000.

[22] http://www.ietf.org/html.charters/.mpls-charter.html.

[23] Chuck Semeria, Juniper Networks, Multi-protocol Label Switching, Enhancing routing in the new public network, 2000.

suppliers of network services, especially if these services include the provision of virtual-WAN services joining branches and remote locations. The following guidelines should be applied during the negotiation of MPLS SLAs to ensure that services live up to the assurance requirements of the converged networks:[24]

- *Site Availability*: Make certain that MPLS is available for all desired locations
- *End-to-End Network Availability*: Inquire about peering relationships for MPLS for network requirements that cross tier 1 carrier boundaries
- *Maximum Time to Restore*: What is the maximum time which will pass before services are restored if they fail, regardless of the SLA limits on availability where refunds kick in?
- *Provisioning*: How fast can new links in new sites be provisioned?

Convergence is often sold as part of an MPLS-managed service. "...in MPLS, compared to frame relay, the unique roles in the pricing structure played by bandwidth reservation mechanisms offer fertile ground for carriers to confuse users. The carriers can roll out bugaboos such as 'future savings' or reduced 'total cost of ownership' rather than make hard savings part of the original bargain. Or they might introduce Class of Service (CoS) pricing that bears little resemblance to other carriers' CoS price structures. Finally, it's usually not prudent to install a big MPLS network right as you're ripping out your frame relay network. Migration costs including the likelihood of running two networks side by side for a period of time are thus a real consideration that must be paid for in order for the MPLS value proposition to pan out."[25]

MPLS users should be aware of the comparative price for the same bandwidth using older technology such as frame relay or ATM. It may be cheaper to buy lots of extra

---

[24] Tips and Traps in Negotiating an MPLS contract, Ben Fox and David Rohde, *Telemanagement*, March 2005 pg 5.

[25] Tips and Traps in Negotiating an MPLS contract, Ben Fox and David Rohde, *Telemanagement*, March 2005 pg 4.

bandwidth on old technology rather than "just enough" on new MPLS circuits.

Detection Safeguards Around Quality of Service Risks:

6. *Network Monitoring Tools.* Network monitoring tools with the ability to track QoS across large organizational networks will become essential controls and safeguards around detection and response to QoS issues. These tools will need the ability to distinguish assets/applications on the network, issue alerts, and ideally re-set QoS prioritizations or bandwidth limits to match QoS requirements with demand on an asset-by-asset basis. Many of these capabilities are currently available today but from disparate vendors with a few interoperability or integration interfaces between them.

Response Safeguards Around Quality of Service Risks:

7. See Network Monitoring Tools above.

Recovery Safeguards Around Quality of Service Risks: No stipulation.

Prevent, detection and response are the three elements around which Location-Implied Functionality safeguards can be planned. The safeguards that have been recommended are presented below.

🔒 Prevent	🔍 Detect	⏱ Respond	➕ Recover
Readiness and Testing Environment (RATE)			
Acceleration of network components			
MPLS			
	Network Monitoring tools		

Asset	Threat Assessment	Risk Assessment	Proposed Controls and Safeguards	Recommendations Residual Risks	Assessment of Safeguards
Data	6	Low	• Patch management	Low	Completely satisfactory
VOIP	9	High	• RATE • Hardware acceleration of processing • MPLS for core networks and WANs • Network monitoring tools	High	Needs improvement; major impediment to deployment outside organization boundaries
Entertainment and Media	6	High		High	Needs improvement; major business impediment
Physical	8	Medium		Low	Satisfactory in most aspects
SCADA	9	High		Low	Satisfactory in most aspects
Banking	9	Low		Low	Satisfactory in most aspects
Facilities	8	Low		Low	Satisfactory in most aspects
Metering	9	Low		Low	Satisfactory in most aspects

Perimeter Stress

Perimeter stress does not result simply because the network perimeter itself becomes larger under convergence; perimeter stress increases because the potential surface area (the exposed surfaces) of the network increases and presents a richer, larger target for threats. As a result, the controls and safeguards associated with the perimeter of a converged network need not just be enhanced but must be re-considered.

Reducing the stress on the perimeter of a converged network is an operational matter. Good procedures and design considerations will go further in reducing perimeter stress than technical solutions involving more devices and capital expenditure.

Some of the issues discussed in this section may be rightly considered technical, but they do not reflect new technology as much as new operational imperatives for employing known techniques and technologies to improved the assurance of converged networks. For instance, the pull toward increased remote access, when coupled with the nature of converged sensitivity, results in some very specific requirements for operational safeguards to preserve the assurance of the IP network.

Prevention Safeguard Around Perimeter Stress Risks:

1. *Standardize on Two-Factor Authentication.* The first safeguard to be re-considered (as opposed to implemented) is the manner in which remote access is granted. Remote access is a problem for all networks because it often presents the most obvious and likely point of attack for malicious outsiders and an especially convenient tool for malicious insiders. To try and limit remote access or even scale it back on a converged network would be an ideal but potentially impractical approach to enhancing assurance for the simple reason that more assets on the network will require more support. Much of this support must be provided by third parties for reasons of efficiency and cost. Convergence drives the requirement for remote access.

Authentication on legitimate remote entry points must be excellent. Two factor authentication should be the minimum standard for remote access to any converged network, not a luxury. Synchronized pseudo-random number generators are one of the best known and widest deployed forms of two-factor authentication. They involve the pairing of a short PIN with a synchronized pseudo-random number generation device. Furthermore, authentication (two-factor or otherwise) should never occur directly upon devices located within the protected network. Authentication should occur on devices within a network DMZ (demilitarized zone). If authentication is successful, connections are then proxied through to a second firewall interface on the perimeter with the protected network. (See Safeguard 6 below for further design guidance for converged networks.)

2. *User Awareness.* The best safeguard to deal with perimeter stress issues such as unauthorized entry points is to engage in a well-administered and scheduled user awareness and training program around security issues associated with converged sensitivity and the inadvertent creation of "back doors" into the network. This safeguard coupled with sanctions for non-compliance will prove highly effective in most organizations and for non-malicious insiders.[26]

3. *Change Control Procedures Around All Changes to Architectures and the Perimeter.* Change control procedures, if implemented correctly, will force all converged assets through the same security processes as Data assets and support common levels of assurance across the assets and their related entry points. What specifically will need to change (from the existing change-control regimes) is that a larger stakeholder group will need to be support change processes because of all the various assets now at stake. For instance, Physical Security and Facilities Management might have a seat at the change-control committee table. Failure to apply change control processes should have serious, management-approved sanctions.

---

[26] SQL Slammer Worm Lessons Learned for Consideration by the Electricity Sector, North American Electricity Reliability Council, June 20, 2003.

4. *Best Practice for Perimeter Design.* The heart of any perimeter safeguard scheme is the firewalls and their support for network segregation and logical security zones. The following list does not necessarily reflect new thinking or new safeguards concerning the security and assurance of the converged ICT perimeter. In fact, it represents well-understood consensus around perimeter "best practice." What is new, however, is that these processes are now being recommended as standard practice not merely "best practice" for converged ICT networks. The distinction between "best practice" and "standard practice" is the difference between "nice to have" and "need to have" (for the purposes of due care and compliance). These techniques, while technical in nature, are really operational design matters.

   a. Use stateful firewalls.[27] A stateful firewall keeps track of connections which originate inside an network and only allows external connections in response to internal requests. Stateful firewalls are complex and might not always support converged applications and assets. But there are always alternatives; for instance, SCADA-aware firewall extensions are available in the open-source world, such as MODBUS-aware extensions for Linux.[28]
   b. Implement combinations of routers and firewalls in-line together rather than using one device for all functions.[29] This has the advantage of allowing simple devices like routers to filter out a wide range of simple attacks that can consume resources and slow performance of a more sophisticated firewall.
   c. Consider use of multiple firewall vendor systems.[30] The advantage of this safeguard is that a potential product vulnerability will not result in a compromise across the entire perimeter. Increasingly this assurance advantage outweighs the issues associated with increased operational costs.

---

[27] NIST 800-58 pg 44.

[28] http://modbusfw.sourceforge.net.

[29] NISCC Good Practice Guide on Firewall Deployment for SCADA and Process Control Networks, National Infrastructure Security Co-ordination Centre, UK Government, Feb 2005, pg 15.

[30] Ibid NISCC, pg 17.

d. Implement independent firewalls for each interface within the DMZ.

e. Do not permit direct, external connections to the critical system networks. No remote connections should bypass the protections afforded by a properly configured firewall. Remote connections should be established into a network DMZ, authenticated, and then allowed to traverse into protected networks thorough a second firewall interface. This includes vendor and remote support communications circuits of any kind.[31]

f. Terminate VPN connections to the critical networks external to the protecting firewall. Do not permit VPN tunneling through the critical system network security perimeter and do not allow VPN split tunneling.[32]

g. Apply "dis-joint" rules. If a protocol is allowed between one critical network or VLAN and the DMZ then it is explicitly *not* allowed the same protocol connects between the DMZ and a separate internal network or VLAN.[33]

h. Deploy purpose-build firewalls and other perimeter safeguards like proxies for assets and applications with especially sensitive QoS requirements like VOIP or video (Entertainment and Media).[34] These firewall may be optimized for UDP and have special hardware-based cryptographic accelerators to support transport level security such as TLS, which is increasingly being used for authentication of VOIP connections.

---

[31] SQL Slammer Worm Lessons Learned for Consideration by the Electricity Sector, North American Electricity Reliability Council, June 20, 2003.

[32] SQL Slammer Worm Lessons Learned for Consideration by the Electricity Sector, North American Electricity Reliability Council, June 20, 2003.

[33] NISCC Good Practice Guide on Firewall Deployment for SCADA and Process Control Networks, National Infrastructure Security Co-ordination Centre, UK Government, Feb 2005, pg 15.

[34] Mark Collier, CTO Securelogix, VOIP Magazine, June 1, 2005, http://www.voip-magazine.com/content/view/108/77/1/1.

i. Implement dedicated, single-purpose firewalls in front of critical pieces of asset infrastructure with very short and simple rule sets. An example is, SIP-specialized firewalls for a VOIP service infrastructure to authenticate devices and connections, a.k.a "Session Border Controllers."[35]

j. For deployment of Entertainment and Media applications, implement upstream rate limits to prevent flooding or other brute-force attacks against infrastructure that is intended to deliver broadband content but receive/manage small volumes of in-bound documentation and accounting data.

k. Implement IP MPLS networks to create virtual private networks for different types of converged content within the network core, or possibly the provider edge router if MPLS has been extended that far.

5. *Telephony Firewalls.* Implement of perimeter security devices to detect and prohibit the tunneling of one type of (unauthorized) communication through a benign channel or, more specifically, telephony-specialized firewalls that can prevent modem or fax connections through VOIP voice-channels. These sorts of threats are well documented in the switched telephony world (search for the word "Linestein®" using any Internet web crawler), and they will become equally prevalent in the converged asset world. Specialized telephony firewalls are available to monitor and track this type of risk and represent a substantial safeguard.[36]

6. *VOIP Border Controllers.* Compartmentalize VOIP infrastructure components[37] the way data infrastructure components are compartmentalized. The primary reason for this—VOIP devices will be accessible to the widest possible range of users and uses, and will serve as an easy source from which to launch attacks or attempts to compromise the assurance of the network and assets.

Regular VOIP devices are segregated and have access to VOIP service-delivery infrastructure (such as media gateways,

---

[35] NIST 800-58, pg 5.
[36] Securelogix Corporation offers an example of this type of capability. http://www.securelogix.com.
[37] IP Telephony Security, MetaGroup Whitepaper, January 2005, pg 4.

call-setup and conferencing servers) only to the extent that they require this access, and VOIP service-delivery infrastructure has access to accounting/billing and directory infrastructure alone while users are denied access entirely. The segregation described above can itself be problematic due to the sensitivity of VOIP to the latency that might be induced by firewalls; for this reason, VOIP-specific session border controllers would be required to affect segregation. The type of session border controller will vary depending on the VOIP implementation—for instance SIP, H.323 or perhaps IAX—and would ideally be selected at the same time as the VOIP infrastructure and be a component of the bid-evaluation criteria.

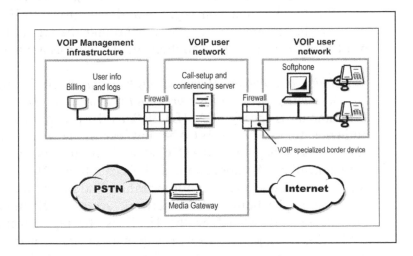

7. *Impact Assessment Checklists.* A safeguard that must be employed around the management of all perimeter devices is carefully defined, tested, and implementation procedures around firewall management. Procedures for firewall changes should start with formal change control requests and approvals but should also include standardized Impact Assessment Checklists to be certain that changes are not considered solely from the perspective of a single asset type (i.e., data) when many other assets are using the same network.

On converged IP networks the range of impacts on all the different assets is likely beyond the point at which a single individual can have sufficient understanding without the benefit of a formalized inventory process. This is to say that Impact Assessment checklists on converged networks should be standard tools developed early and maintained on a scheduled basis. Impact Assurance Checklist need not be complex tools; they should be a moderately detailed relationship model of which assets rely upon which network devices and components (such as firewalls, routers, ect.). When a change is planned or implemented to a network component, a check should be done of all related assets to ensure that unintended impacts have not occurred. In the "old" IP data world we became accustomed to thinking of network devices as relatively simple and thus prediction of the impacts to be almost intuitive. This sort of thinking will scale poorly in converged ICT environments.

8. *Fixed Mobile Union (FMU) Controls:* The increased complexity of networks in a converged world will drive FMU and increase the requirement for controls around the logical movement from one network to another. FMU controls are about:

   Defining a Common Means of Authentication, Authorization, and Accounting Between Enterprise and Carrier Networks: IMS IMS standards specify DIAMETERR as the primary means of authentication between WLAN and carrier networks. Most enterprises today use RADIUS-based means of granting Authentication, Authorization, and Accounting. DIAMETER is an AAA (authentication, authorization and accounting) protocol for applications such as network access or IP mobility. DIAMETER is defined by the IETF as the replacement for RADIUS, its objective is to provide a base protocol that can be extended to AAA services for new access technologies. DIAMETER is intended to work in both local and roaming AAA situations.[38]

   The name is a pun on the name of its competing/predecessor protocol RADIUS (a diameter is twice the radius). DIAMETER is not directly backwards compatible, but provides an upgrade path for RADIUS. The main differences are that DIAMETER:

   - Uses reliable transport protocols (TCP or SCTP, not UDP)
   - Uses transport level security (IPSEC or TLS)
   - Has transition support for RADIUS

---

[38] Wikipedia, *Diameter Article.*

- Has larger address space for AVPs (Attribute Value Pairs) and identifiers (32-bit instead of 8-bit)
- Is a peer-to-peer protocol, not client-server: supports server-initiated messages
- Is both stateful and stateless—both models can be used
- Has dynamic discovery of peers (using DNS SRV and NAPTR)
- Has capability negotiation
- Supports application layer acknowledgments, defines failover methods and state machines (RFC 3539)
- Has error notification
- Is easier to extend because new commands and attributes can be defined
- Has support for accounting built in

Until such time as enterprises and network providers have widely deployed DIAMETER, IMS network equipment vendors who are building the IMS defined CSCF and P-CSCF (Call Session Control Function server and Proxy CSCF) network elements will continue to deploy with other extensible means of authentication, for instance 802.1x and non 802.1x networks (e.g., EAP-SIM). Once 802.1x is widely deployed in existing enterprise and hotspot networks, the implementation of full IMS standard AAA will proceed.

Defining a Standard Means of Security and Remote Management on Mobile Devices. IMS does not define encryption standards or remote management capability, but leverages IEEE Standards for noncellular network security. As of this writing, organizations are merely beginning to deploy dual-mode WiFi/Cellular devices. As the number of employees using an enterprise-provided mobile device increases, the importance of developing enterprise mobile security standards also increases.

Many organizations implement dual-mode mobile devices to improve work-force productivity. Increasingly they demand devices that support existing organizational security controls, such as VPN deployments, encryption technologies, and management features, such as the ability to remotely wipe clean lost or stolen devices. Most smart phone vendors have been slow to provide remote device management software, or to support multiple device encryption methods.[39]

Extending Authentication Mid-Session to Allow for Seamless Handover Between Access Networks. One feature of emerging Fixed Mobile Union (FMU) services that highlights the difficulties of securing converged networks is the issue of handover. In the example of an "organization hosted" IP-PBX/Cellular service, the device must be able to authenticate to both the enterprise WiFi/PBX environment as well as the cellular carrier environment. Today, Extensible Authentication Protocol (EAP) variants such as EAP-SIM (Subscriber Identity Module) are common methods to support authentication/registration of devices as they move from WiFi to Cellular, and vice versa. EAP-SIM and other authentication methods must evolve to support the 802.1x methods and DIAMETER as specified in the IMS and IETF standards. This means that solutions used in early FMU solutions must be upgradable to a standards-based solutions. Organizations contemplating hosted/managed FMU solutions must ensure that the service provider upgrades to standards-based solutions. However, it is the equipment manufacturers that are really setting the pace for the deployment of standards-based FMU. Any assumptions about the availability of FMU equipment with wide-scale interoperability must be based upon equipment vendors commitments.

Potential New Vulnerabilities as Messages from Cellular and Public WiFi HotSpot Networks Are Delivered into Enterprise WiFi Services. Closely related to the standards issue is Cellular Signaling and Message delivery into organizational WiFi infrastructures. Until now, organizations have relied on Firewall, Anti-Virus (AV), and Anti-Spam (AS) software to prevent malicious instructions from entering through corporate ICT systems. With the advent of FMU, new threats have emerged as cellular messaging instructions are passed to dual-mode devices operating on the organizational network. These

---

[39] Network World Executive Guide, *Questions Around SmartPhone Security*, Denise Dubie and Phil Hochmuth.

forms of network traffic are especially difficult to identify and filter because they rely on the telephone number as the primary addressing scheme and alternate network interface. This information may bypass typical server-based AV and AS implementations.

This issue is amplified because in the (unfamiliar) cellular signaling world, distinguishing legitimate from illegitimate Short Message Service (SMS) or Multi-Media SMS (MMS) messages is far from being a well understood capability like AV or AS. In addition, some of the dual mode WiFi/Cellular services rely on SMS as a means to pass roaming information between the cellular and WiFi networks. This presents a new and potentially very dangerous vulnerability to denial of service attacks against organizational infrastructure. Developing the means to prevent such attacks will rely on new levels of cooperation between the enterprise and the carriers.

Detection Safeguards Around Perimeter Stress Risks:

9. Telephony firewalls will automatically alert security staff of contraventions in security policy.
10. VOIP border controllers can be integrated with IDS/IPS service to alert around suspicious loads or activities on otherwise dedicated VOIP ports and protocols.
11. Sustained monitoring for unauthorized entry points. While this may seem like obvious advice—and it is obvious—it is the most frequently ignored operational safeguard. Why are unauthenticated entry points ignored? For several reasons: 1) most managers do not have any visibility into the scale of the problem and underestimate perimeter stress as a threat, 2) the impact of unauthorized entry points is often inconclusive because security incidents cannot easily be tracked back to those entry points in many cases, and 3) managers do not ask the questions (i.e., ignore the problem) because they simply do not have any budget to deal with the findings.

A detection safeguard appropriate to converged networks and assets deals with the management of unauthorized entry points specifically, both ingress and egress. These devices must be discovered and shut down. This capability must involve not only fixed line entry points such as illicit modems and VPN devices, but unauthorized wireless (WiFi, WiMax, Bluetooth, etc) entry points as well. The assumption must be made that these unauthenticated entry points will pop up and disappear rapidly and repeatedly, therefore sustained monitoring of fixed line and especially wireless environments is currently the only answer.

Response Safeguards Around Perimeter Stress Risks:

12.   VOIP border controllers can be integrated with network-centric security tools to automatically restrict traffic from specific sources or devices.

13.   Computer Incident Response Teams (CIRTs) are evolving to address not only threats related to data assets but all Triple Play and Transparent assets too. These teams should have the ability to respond to the appearance of unauthorized entry-points by tracking and removing these devices from the organizational network on short notice. They should have the necessary tools and training to do this. In the case of fixed-lined entry points, this will involve the use of packet-sniffing devices and the ability to tap into and trace network cabling, a tedious but relatively simple process. In the even more serious unauthorized wireless entry points, special radio tracking equipment should be deployed to CIRT units. This equipment is simpler and cheaper than one would expect ($100s not $1000s) and should be a baseline capability for CIRT services.

Recovery Safeguards Around Perimeter Stress Risks: No stipulation.

Prevent, detection, and respond are the three elements around which Perimeter Stress Safeguards can be planned. The safeguards that have been recommended are presented below.

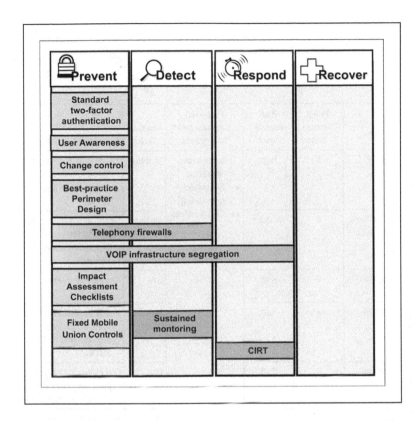

Asset			Recommendations		
	Threat Assess-ment	Risk Assess-ment	Proposed Controls and Safeguards	Residual Risks	Assessment of Safeguards
Data	9	High	• Two-factor authentica-tion • Training and awareness • Implement best practices • Impact	Low	Completely satisfactory; data are a much better understood asset relative to the converging assets. The proposed safeguards are all designed based upon data-asset experiences

(Continued)

Asset	Threat Assess-ment	Risk Assess-ment	Recommendations		
			Proposed Controls and Safeguards	Residual Risks	Assessment of Safeguards
VOIP	9	High	assurance checklists • Sustained monitoring • CIRT services	Medium	Needs improvement; see "Green Protocols, Architectures and Stacks"
Entertainment and Media	8	Medium		Medium	Needs improvement; see "Green Protocols, Architectures and Stacks"
Physical	9	High		Low	Satisfactory in most aspects
SCADA	9	High		Medium	Needs improvement; see "Green Protocols, Architectures and Stacks"
Banking	9	High		Low	Completely satisfactory; good end-point and network security already
Facilities	9	High		Low	Satisfactory in most aspects; see "Green Protocols, Architectures and Stacks"
Metering	9	High		Low	Satisfactory in most aspects; see "Green Protocols, Architectures and Stacks"

Technical Threats

Technical controls focus on security controls that the [converged network] system executes. The controls can provide automated protection for unauthorized access or misuse, facilitate detection of security violations, and support security requirements for applications and data.[40]

Electrical Environment Sensitivity

The impact of interrupted power supply is a fairly obvious consideration to anyone experienced in designing applications systems and services, and a wide variety of safeguards are available to preserve power during disruptions. The safeguards range from small, shoe box–sized UPS devices that will protect against short term brown-outs or keep a computer running long enough to gracefully shut it down. On the other side of the spectrum are large diesel generators that will automatically activate once the power from the electricity grid fails, and keep the entire building running (or critical components like elevators and/or data centers). The simple option is cheap but of little use in preserving assurance of the asset it is supporting; the large generator option is expensive, very expensive.

As discussed in Chapter 3, under convergence all assets end up on the same physical network. If the power fails and the network drops, an organization stands to lose all the converged assets at the same instant (Fig. 2). There is no redundancy available through legacy, standalone networks like the old internal phone system. Compounding this problem, most of the network devices are in-line and become single points of failure because the loss of power to one of these devices might cut off large segments of the network. Similarly, most end-point devices like VOIP phones will not currently function without building power, even if the network remains available.

Intensifying the power failure issue is the requirement that the in-line devices are also required to be physically dispersed throughout the organization's facilities, which means that they cannot take advantage of the UPS capabilities that might be built into a data center. As a result, most organizations do not place electrical supply safeguards on these devices because the cost of individual UPS devices would be both prohibitive and probably ineffective—ineffective

---

[40] NIST 800-26 pg A-43.

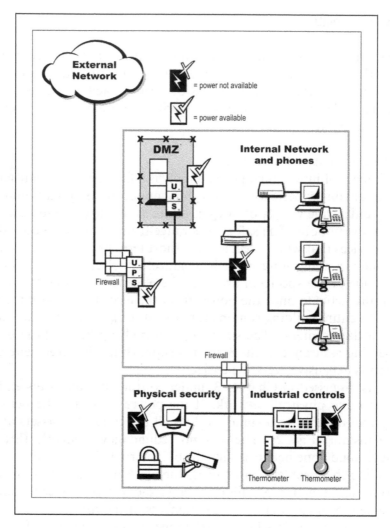

Figure 2 Power failure impact on converged networks.

because UPS devices require maintenance, monitoring and testing on a frequent basis and there is a very good chance that this will be neglected and that these devices will simply fail when needed. Such failures represent a typical scenario.

Another alternative is to leave these devices hooked directly into the building power supply as they are currently, and try and provide UPS to the entire building with generators. This is a hugely expensive prospect, generally only seen in the most critical operational environments.

Prevention Safeguards Around Electrical Sensitivity Risks:

1. *Power over Ethernet (PoE)*. A more affordable safeguard for converged networks that may be implemented incrementally is to adopt Power over CAT5 Ethernet (PoE). (CAT5 is the standard Local Area Network—LAN—cable.) PoE is a means of running the power necessary for remote in-line devices directly over the LAN cabling. PoE begins with a CAT5 "Injector" device that inserts DC Voltage onto the cable. Devices that are not built to handle PoE can be converted to PoE with a DC "Picker" or "Tap." The Tap removes the DC voltage from the CAT5 cable, and makes the power available to the device through the native DC power jack. The Tap sits on the physical cable in front of the device and "removes" the DC power from the ethernet cable before it reaches the LAN interface jack of the device (Fig. 3).

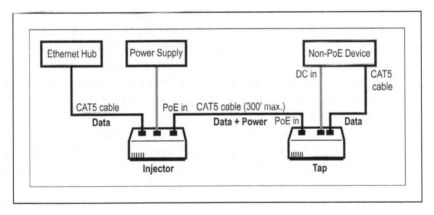

Figure 3 PoE with Injector and Tap.

- The IEEE has a PoE standard called IEEE 802.3af. Not all PoE equipment vendors have implemented this specification, so be sure that all PoE equipment meets the same specification.
- There are limits to the cable length of PoE. The IEEE standard utilizes a higher voltage (48) for greater range but lower voltage and therefore PoE ranges are available and may be appropriate where cable length is not a major requirement.[41]

---

[41] http://www.hyperlinktech.com/web/what_is_poe.php.

The voltage requirements based upon cable length can be calculated using some simple tools that are available on the
Internet.[42]

- Devices should come equipped with both surge protection and
  electromagnetic interference (EMI) filters to prevent as little
  interference and corruption of data as possible as the IP packets and power share the physical medium.The advantage of
  this approach is that remote devices can be powered and managed from more centralized locations for lower cost. For
  instance, a large UPS device could be located in the telecom
  closet or LAN room and will power the remote in-line and
  end-point devices during a power outage for an entire LAN
  segment or multiple LAN segments (Fig. 4).

  Deploying yet more remote, in-line (the PoE Injectors and
  the Taps) devices is neither an elegant nor long term answer
  to the problem of power interruptions. This represents more
  equipment to manage and more potential points of failure.
  The real solution will be for manufacturers of converged
  ICT network devices to start incorporating PoE capabilities
  into the in-line and end-point devices which will allow UPS
  services to be extended across facilities to wherever the LAN
  cabling is present. The alternative of "whole building" UPS
  is cost prohibitive.

  A counter-consideration to the deployment of PoE is the
  impact of network noise on the converged assets using the
  same physical wire for IP. Network noise can be introduced
  by a wide variety of factors, of which PoE is one, and must
  be managed in order to avoid degrading the performance of
  the network past the point of usability for some of the
  converged assets. Recall that many in-line devices like switches
  and routers will filter out network noise from one physical
  span to the other, but these devices may not filter out the errors
  and corrupted packets that result from this noise. The *noise*
  may not bleed across network spans but the *errors* will pass
  through the in-line devices.

2. *Power from Central Offices (CO)*. Different than PoE but similar in effect is the use of power from telecom central offices (CO)

---

[42] http://www.gweep.net/~sfoskett/tech/poecalc.html.

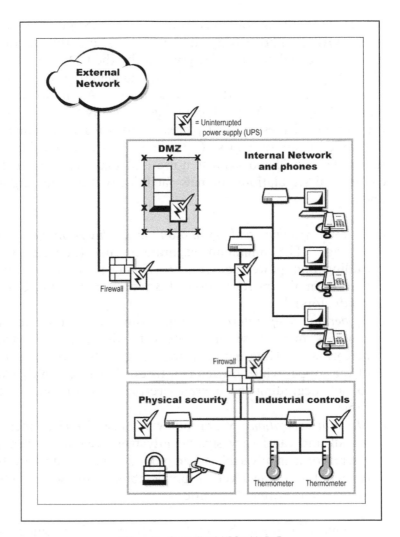

Figure 4 Centralized UPS with PoE.

to run devices. This is the power that comes in over the twisted-pair copper line to the building or home. This is also the power source that has given Plain Old Telephone Service (POTS) the 99.999% availability and assurance that most people in North American and Europe have grown up with. COs are highly redundant and well-provisioned hubs for telecommunications and are generally set-up to continue operations when the rest of the world around them has stopped. This continuance of service is extended all the way to end-point device (phones).

One of the evolving solutions from some service providers is to offer VOIP telephone with all the features and toll discounts and with the end-point device powered by the CO.

3. *Cable Deployment.* Cabling is the fundamental physical medium of much of our IP network traffic. As networks are impacted by the effects of converged sensitivity the physical deployment of these critical pieces of infrastructure should be considered from all angles. The following electrical safeguards should be considered against noise and may represent useful contractual stipulations for new facilities or those undergoing upgrade.[43]

- *Correct spacing and insulation from high-voltage power cabling*: "The minimum separation rule (between LAN cabling and power sources) is 1.5 inches for every 100 V (with a minimum separation of 3 inches from NEC Class 1 conductors)."
- *Moderate temperatures*: Temperature variations in the conduits may cause problems with the cable's electrical performance. High temperatures increase the DC resistance of the copper while low temperatures will cause cable jackets to fail, degrading the overall electrical performance of the cable.
- *Moderate vibrations*: Vibrations will cause RJ-45 connectors to fail and rates vary significantly from vendor to vendor. Therefore it is advisable to employ a single vendor product to maintain some level of predictability into when failure might occur in remote locations.

The impact between the implementation of PoE safeguards and the interference that power might cause to network traffic is very subjective to the assets deployed and the QoS requirements of these assets.

---

[43] Ethernet: Surviving the Manufacturing Environment White Paper, Bob Lousnbury, Physical Layer engineer, Rockwell Automation, May 2001.

Detection Safeguards Around Electrical Sensitivity Risks:

4. *Security Event Management (SEM)*. Security Event Management (SEM) tools and systems will have the ability to apply heart-beat monitoring against critical devices and consolidate logs from network monitoring tools. One of the most likely causes of failure of a device and its heart beat is simple power failure, not hacking. Similarly, a monitored increase in data errors from a network segment is usually an indicator of a problem with the physical deployment or degradation of the ethernet cable. SEM services can be tuned to alert on these sorts of events and allow for response services to be initiated.

Response Safeguards Around Electrical Sensitivity Risks: No stipulation.

Recovery Safeguards Around Electrical Sensitivity Risks: No stipulation.

Prevent and detection are the two elements around which Electrical Sensitivity safeguards can be planned. The safeguards that have been recommended are presented below.

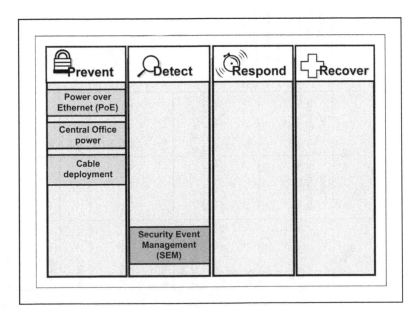

General Environment Security

Asset	Threat Assessment	Risk Assessment	Recommendations		
			Proposed Controls and Safeguards	Residual Risks	Assessment of Safeguards
Data	9	Medium	• LAN-based UPS couple with PoE • CO Power • Cable management • Best practice perimeter design • SEM	High	Needs improvement • End-point devices are often desktop computers and they cannot be sustained with PoE
VOIP	9	High		Medium/low	Needs improvement • End-point devices do not natively support PoE, require additional in-line devices • CO power provides significantly reduced availability risks
Entertainment and Media	9	Medium		Low	Completely satisfactory; emergency services and digital rights not threatened by outage
Physical	9	High		Medium	Needs improvement • End-point devices do not natively support PoE, require additional in-line devices
SCADA	9	High		Medium	Needs improvement • End-point devices do not natively support PoE, require additional in-line devices
Banking	9	Medium		Low	Completely satisfactory; end-point devices are outside organizational (FI) controls and central processing infrastructure is hardened
Facilities	9	High		Medium	Needs improvement • End-point devices do not natively support PoE, require additional in-line devices
Metering	9	Medium		Low	Completely satisfactory; end point devices are outside organizational (FI) controls and central processing infrastructure is hardened

Soft Devices: Talented Mimics

Soft devices are software programs which utilize the native processing power of the host computer to mimic the functionality of "hard devices" and simply run on commodity platforms like PC devices or laptops. Implementing controls for soft devices is exceedingly difficult because these devices can be installed and uninstalled with ease, and introduced into the converged network with a minimum of effort, especially if the host device is already allowed on the network. For the most part this will also mean that unauthorized soft devices will probably be introduced by either misguided or malicious insiders because they already have devices on the network. We should not to minimalize the potential for entirely new and entirely unauthorized devices to be connected to the internal converged network—this is definitely a possibility, which was covered in the Perimeter Stress section. For a malicious entity attempting to engage in unauthorized activity the tool of choice would be a laptop-type device loaded with a wide range of software devices: soft phones, PLC-emulators, monitoring devices, traffic generators, and just about every conceivable type of converged device.

Protection Safeguards Around Soft-devices Risks:

1. *Limit Device-to-Device Connections and Interchange.* Firewalls on the perimeter and centralized services should only allow connections from specifically allowed, internal (or external) IP addresses (or possibly MAC address) using only a specific protocol. These capabilities involve detailed analysis of the information packet including checking the payload for the protocol in use to be sure it matched the application on a given port. These system are often referred to as "Intrusion Prevention Services" (IPS). (MAC addresses cannot be used as a control once the data have traversed a layer-3 switch, because the ethernet device information from the source interface has been supplanted by the switch's MAC address.)

2. *Internal Switching and Routing Rules.* Such rules only allow network traffic from specifically configured device addresses (Medium Access Control addresses or MACs) to send and receive designated protocols within the LAN segment. For instance, only the MACs assigned to desktop hard-phones may use SIP-specific ports.

3. *Session Security*. Use session security (such as IPSec or TLS) between assets and end-point devices to make observation of traffic and configuration information difficult for an unauthorized soft device.
4. *End-Point Authentication*. This is discussed elsewhere in this chapter.

It should be noted that safeguard 1 best reflects the recently popularized notion of "intrusion prevention", which is generally about performing as much analysis on the data as possible before it reaches its destination to determine if it is malicious. Similarly, Safeguard 3 attempts to create VPN-type connections between all end points, and central assets. This safeguard should be implemented with caution because security incidents will become much more difficult to detect if they are obscured (from good guys and bad guys alike) within a VPN.

Detection Safeguards Around Soft-Devices Risks:

5. *IPS/IDS*. A variety of network equipment vendors are marketing products around "network-based" security, where devices on the network monitor the presence of unauthorized devices or activities—"network-based" meaning that these devices service both the device and the network as a whole as opposed to server-based or host-based security like firewalls or anti-virus that focus on information arriving and leaving the host-cum-bastion device. These products are sometimes called Intrusion Prevention Services (IPS) but in fact might be closer to an "empowered" form of Intrusion Detection Services (IDS).

    - *Intrusion Prevention Services (IPS)*: IPS can be either host based or network based, but in most cases it is network based, located at an ingress points such as a firewall. IPS will attempt to inspect the content of each packet down to the payload level and make a decision based on pre-defined rules if the packet is part of a developing attack or compromise. The decision the IPS is empowered to make may be to kill the content, come what may.
    - *Intrusion Detection Services (IDS)*: IDS also can be either host based or network based. IDS is normally located on the network and issues alerts if traffic patterns deviate from normal or match known attack signatures/patterns.

The capabilities of network-based security will vary from vendor to vendor, but will likely include the ability to detect newly arrived devices through MAC address checks and the correlation of a traffic profile against know MACs. In this way they can alert administrators to potential security incidents. And of course these products will also perform more typical IDS services independent of MAC/IP address monitoring, such as pattern, heuristic, and anomaly detection on network traffic as a whole with alerts around unusual events.

6. *End-Point Security.* End-point security again may play a role through the detection of failed authentication attempts by otherwise "normal" looking devices on the network, indicating that address spoofing (mimicking) is occurring by unauthorized soft devices.
7. *Security Event Monitoring.* SEM services will show their true value in their potential to correlate events from IPS/IDS and End-point authentication failure. While all of these services themselves will generate a large number of false positives, a correlation of events across all these detection techniques would be a much clearer indication of a true security event.

A combination of detection techniques has many advantages over the status quo in network security, which is heavily reliant upon perimeter security devices. But it does not represent a complete solution for several reasons: first, again, no end-point security is incorporated, leaving the end-point vulnerable and entirely dependant upon the network for security. Second, network-based security results in additional, complex devices to buy, manage, and potentially fail. The price of the network alone climbs. Third, IDS systems are known to generate a staggering amount of false-positive results on mundane Data networks. The affect of converged assets onto an IP-based network is virtually unknown at this time and will probably generate even more false positives, and require subject matter experts to configure and maintain. Caveat emptor.

Safeguard 5: IPS/IDS network-based security includes monitoring of new devices and the isolation of these devices pending administrator investigation. This is a valuable advancement, however, like IDS, this technology is largely untested in highly converged environments and may result in diminishing returns relative to investment requirements as a result, Safeguard 6: End-point security is perhaps an especially useful feature given that it pushes some of the assurance capabilities out of centralized network devices as a hedge against massive failure/breach on the centralized components.

Response: Safeguards Around Response to Soft-Device Risks.

8.   *Network-Based Security*. Network-based security (depending on the vendor) should include the ability to isolate suspect devices on the network through on-the-fly switching/routing configuration changes that deny traffic to and from the device, ideally at the nearest LAN switch.

9.   *Computer Incident Response Team (CIRT)*. There services are coordinated and skilled human resources with a combination of tools, and authority to rapidly react to security incidents related to the converged network. CIRT services can range from "volunteer firefighter" arrangements with employees, to dedicated and trained staff with skills in not only system patching and recovery procedures but also forensics. Methodologies for the definition and management of CIRT services are available from a variety of sources such as SANS[44] and NIST[45] for use by entities that wish to create a CIRT service. Alternately, CIRT services can often be purchased from security service providers under a wide variety of pricing schemes.

Both Safeguards 8 and 9 represent good value to organizations supporting converged assets and networks. Safeguard 8: CIRT Services particularly is available to just about any organization regardless of budget, and plays a large role in the overall Disaster Recovery and Business Continuity Program as a whole.

Recovery: Safeguards Around Soft-Sevice Risks.

10.   *Computer Incident Response Team (CIRT)* Service. This will play a dual role in mitigating threats from soft devices and fundamental intrusions into the converged network, because CIRT service includes analysis of what happened and the recommendation of how processes and procedures need to

---

[44] http://www.sans.org.

[45] NIST 800-61, Computer Security Incident Handling Guide, 2004.

be improved and adjusted. In many cases, intrusions due to soft devices will be the result of weak policies and procedures and fundamental human error. Tracing the chain of events around soft-device intrusion back to policy and procedure is well beyond the capability of anything but a human at this point.

Prevent, detect, respond and recovery are the four elements around which soft-device safeguards can be planned. The safeguards that have been recommended are presented below.

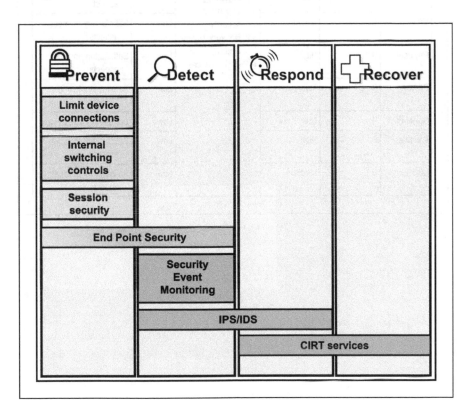

Asset	Threat Assessment	Risk Assessment	Proposed Controls and Safeguards	Residual Risks	Assessment of Safeguards
Data	NA	NA	• Firewalls	NA	NA
VOIP	9	High	• Internal switching	Low	Satisfactory in most aspects
IPTV	6	Medium	• End-point security	Low	Satisfactory in most aspects
Physical	9	High	• Network-based security	Low	Satisfactory in most aspects
SCADA	9	Medium	• CIRT services	Low	Satisfactory in most aspects
Banking	9	Low		Low	Completely satisfactory
Facilities	8	High		Low	Satisfactory in most aspects
Metering	9	Medium		Low	Satisfactory in most aspects

Green Protocols, Stacks, and Architectures

Introducing safeguards around poorly designed or poorly implemented protocols, stacks, and architectures can be a challenge if for no other reason than these flaws are often not apparent until the damage has been done. This also makes the adoption of these safeguards especially important under converged networks, because the business interdependencies among converged assets mean that a flaw resulting in a vulnerability in one asset inherently exposes the other assets to risks.

Protection: Safeguards Around Green Protocols, Stacks and Architecture Risks.

1. *Threat Risk Assessments (TRAs)*. Performance of formalized Threat-Risk Assessments (TRAs) on all new applications, systems, and services coming on to the converged network should systemically expose risks related to flaws in protocols, stacks, and architectures. TRAs should output qualitative metrics around the risks presented and provide a consistent measure against which management can make decisions to accept or reject risks. Performance of TRAs are categorized as technical exercises for the purposes of this discussion because they normally involve granular technical assessments of network and device features.

2. *Mandate Application Firewalls*. Mandatory implementation of application-level filtering firewalls to support the newly converged protocols and prohibit the use or opening of General Service Ports. For instance, firewalls may not be aware of the converging protocols (especially in Transparent convergence) that have a foundation in proprietary stand-alone industrial networks, especially SCADA protocols. Before these devices are converged onto the IP network, managers should ensure that there is some sort of vendor support for application-level firewall filtering. If this cannot be supplied by the device-manufacturer as a firewall plugin, then the firewall vendor should be queried about support. If no one can provide application-level filtering, then the devices network may be converged onto IP but without physical connections to the converged network. (Increasing, maintain a physically distinct and expensive network.)

3. *High Availability DHCP and Directory Services*. These services should be implemented as hardened, high-availability systems if

they service two or more converged assets. As discussed in Chapter 3, these network services must not be taken for granted as they sometimes have been in the past.

4. *Separate Logical Networks for Different Converged Assets.* Employ VLAN technology to segregate assets. For instance, a different subnet for VOIP. The main problem associated with this safeguard is that, new core networking hardware may be required to support these sorts of logical, architectural safeguards because of the traffic and switching volumes that will be generated by converged applications.[46]

5. *Maintain Open and Clear Communications with Supplier and Vendors.* All of the above safeguards are both effective and relatively easy to implement on converged network but not always without additional costs; as is the case in item 4.

Detection: Safeguards Around Green Protocols, Stacks, and Architecture Risks.

6. *Security Event Management (SEM) Systems and Services.* Testing of new versions of vendor-implementations of protocols is not a practical suggestion due to cost. The skills required to determine if and where a protocol flaw exists are scarce and, in fact, most such flaws are discovered by accident or coincidence rather than through methodical testing. Organizations should keep inventories of the protocols they support and the vendor applications and devices upon which they are currently deployed. In that way, when a vulnerability is announced it is possible to determine specifically which assets are impacted and what actions are mandated in terms of remediation. This sort of functionality is part of Security Event Management systems and services.

7. *Network Monitoring Tools.* These tools are increasingly available and focused on the upper layers of the network, focusing on the real-time analysis of protocol and payload information. In the future, these types of tools will prove invaluable for the purposes of flagging architectural flaws that result in conflicts between converged applications, especially conflicts between real-time applications using UDP and near-time applications running TCP.

---

[46] NIST 800-58, pg 89.

8. *Open-Source Security Information Collection and Analysis.* "Open-source" information refers to data that can be gathered on the open internet without charge, from mailing lists to web pages to chat rooms to IRC channels. Open-source analysis tools are being developed and made available on a managed service basis that scan publicly available sources of vulnerability information (such as vendor sites, bug-traq mailing lists, blogs, chat rooms) for emerging information about vulnerabilities related to different devices and platforms. When tuned to the organization's inventory of critical end-point devices, open-source analysis becomes a useful vulnerability detection and forecasting tool.

9. *RATE.* Implement a Readiness and Testing Environment (RATE) within which patches and upgrades can be tested prior to upgrading critical production systems.[47] This is not as simple as it sounds. Many mangers may be surprised at the difference between what they consider good, cautious implementation techniques and what is, in fact, a truly appropriate testing and implementation regime in light of the converged sensitivity of the IP network and the impact on assurance of Green protocols, stacks and architectures. See Chapter 5: Managing Assurance for a discussion of application implementation and testing regimes that would be appropriate to converged networks.

***Response*:** Safeguards Around Green Protocols, Stacks, and Architecture Risks.

10. *SEM Systems and Services.* These play a significant role in response through their capability to facilitate the deployment of patches related to vendors' products and devices impacted by a flaw in a protocol, stack or architecture.

11. *CIRT Services.* These services will allow for the rapid assessment of the criticality of flaws in protocols, stacks, and architectures and the implementation and execution of response plans. A CIRT team may become the focal point and accountable entity in the event that a serious protocol or architectural flaw is discovered and remediation must occur both rapidly and complexly.

---

[47] SQL Slammer Worm Lessons Learned for Consideration by the Electricity Sector, North American Electricity Reliability Council, June 20, 2003.

Both these safeguards should be a significant part of the assurance of a converged network. The extent to which both safeguards 9 and 10 are resourced is dependant upon the organization's risk tolerance and the threats faced; there a wide variety of different implementation options from luxury to basic, from in-house to out-sourced managed services for both SEM and CIRT.

Recovery: Safeguards Around Green Protocols, Stacks, and Architecture Risks.
12.   *CIRT Services*. CIRT services should support the recovery of systems, services, and applications, including forensic services and procedures if required.
13.   *Feedback Loop into Procurement Decisions*. The outcome of any incident related to protocol, stack, or architecture flaws should clearly documented, including:

- Assets involved
- Assets impacted
- Vendor response (time, comprehensiveness)

This outcome should be logged and used for decisions around procurement/upgrades/evergreening in the future.

Prevent, detect, respond, and recovery are the four elements around which protocol, stack and architectural safeguards can be planned. The safeguards which have been recommended are presented below.

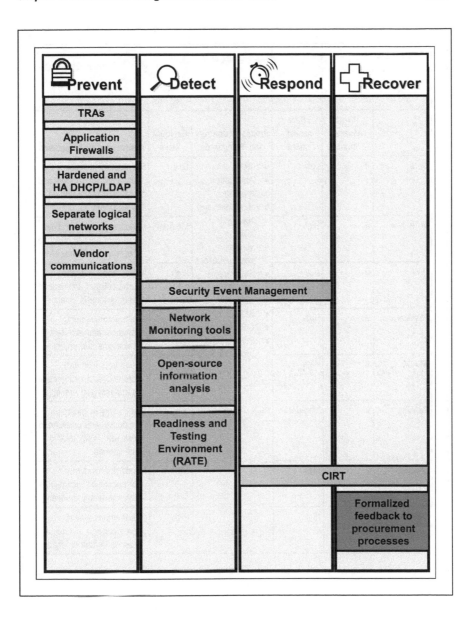

| Asset | Threat Assess- ment | Risk Assess- ment | Recommendations | | |
			Proposed Controls and Safeguards	Residual Risks	Assessment of Safeguards
Data	9	Low	• TRAs • Application firewalls • Hardened and HA DHCP / LDAP • Vendor communications • Separate logical networks • SEM • CIRT • Procurement feedback loop	Low	Satisfactory in most aspects; well understood risk with many related safeguards
VOIP	9	High		Medium	Needs improvement; final protocol and architecture standards still emerging
IPTV	9	High		High	Needs Improvement; protocol and architecture standards still emerging
Physical	9	High		High	Needs improvement; protocol and architecture standards still emerging
SCADA	9	High		High	Needs improvement; protocol and architecture standards still emerging
Banking	9	Medium		Low	Satisfactory in most aspects; well understood risk with many related safeguards
Facilities	9	High		High	Needs improvement; protocol and architecture standards still emerging
Metering	9	High		High	Needs improvement; protocol and architecture standards still emerging

End Point Security

End point security is a big part of the future of convergence and of the assurance of converged assets. To date, end points have largely relied upon perimeter security to do most of the heavy lifting around network-based attacks, anti-virus and anti-spam, authentication management, access controls, etc. This situation is rapidly changing under convergence— "changing" as in "no longer satisfactory" —because convergence dramatically increases the number of assets and end points in the network: the more assets, the more end points, and therefore, the more entry points to the network; the more end points, the more potential for a misconfigured, defective, or malicious device to impact the whole network.

The internal network may be a Walled Garden as discussed earlier but the garden will still have snake and spiders. End-point devices will need to cope with threats independently: They may not be successful against all threats, but must certainly offer resistance where previously the status quo was abject surrender if a threat agent made it past the perimeter.

The major issues opposing the hardening of end-point devices are not easily overcome and reflect serious engineering or business challenges; for instance:

- Limited memory or processing power. For instance, cryptographic key management is routinely lacking from the transport security of converged applications.
- Limited battery power
- Costs difficult to justify in view of expected amortization

Protection: Safeguards Around End-Point Device Risks.
1. *Session Security.* Implementation of session encryption between end points and central services, or from end point to end point. For instance, NIST recommends IPSec tunneling with VOIP.[48]
2. *End Point Authentication.* Implementation of end-point authentication between end points and central services, or from end point to end point. In this case, encryption may not be applied to information exchanges, but the connection is authenticated.
3. *Utilization of Static IP Address for Converged Devices and Applications where Possible.* If not required, do not use DHCP

---

[48] NIST 800-58 pg 6.

since it introduces another potential point of attack and failure
into the convergence architecture.

4. *Device Proxies.* Introduction of converged security/proxy
    devices in front of simpler, legacy devices. For instance, a com-
    mon means of extending the life of legacy equipment while
    converging these devices on IP is to implement Analogue-to-
    Digital converters as the interface between the end-point
    device and the converged network. These devices could also
    provide enhanced assurance around end-point devices if they
    were hardened and designed to support some authentication
    and encryption capabilities. Conversely, these devices can
    introduce wildly new vulnerabilities if not hardened and
    secured, as discussed in Chapter 3.

5. *End-Point Hardening.* Where possible:

    - Authenticate and automate firmware/software upgrade
      processes (in-field)
    - Enable logging or administrative operations if possible
    - Enable heart-beat monitoring with end points
    - Install host-based firewalls

6. *End-Point Administration.* Where possible:

    - Be certain that any end-point passwords are changed from
      manufacturer defaults and changed regularly, especially if
      they must be shared by necessity, i.e., SCADA (no memory
      for user accounts)
    - Disable remote access features or
    - Disable local administration

Safeguard 1 above, while prescribed by an authoritative
source, likely possesses a wide variety of problems concerning issues
from latency to lawful access. Furthermore, point-to-point encryption will not address availability issues (other than reducing vulner-
ability-related compromise from unauthorized access) as noted
earlier, encrypting all traffic in UPA will also increase loads,
decrease availability, a reduce the effectiveness of IPS/IDS services.
For these reasons, end point to end point is not recommended on a
universal basis.

Detection: Safeguards Around End-Point Device Risks.

7. *Security Event Management (SEM)* Systems and Services. SEM services may include the monitoring of end-point devices for heart-beats and activities that indicate normal functioning. Conversely, they will also alarm administrators if end-point behaviors go outside normal operating parameters. SEM services may also preserve logs for end-point devices, central servers, and perimeter devices for later analysis for unauthorized or unusual events or patterns, and issue alarms.

8. *Open-Source Security Information Collection and Analysis.* "Open-source" information refers to data that can be gathered on the open Internet without charge, from mailing lists to web pages to chat rooms to IRC channels. Open-source analysis tools are being developed and made available on a managed-service basis, that scan publicly available sources of vulnerability information (such as vendor sites, bug-traq mailing lists, blogs, chat rooms) for emerging information about vulnerabilities related to different devices and platforms. When tuned to the organization's inventory of critical end-point devices, open-source analysis becomes a useful vulnerability detection and forecasting tool.

9. *Network-Based Security.* A variety of network equipment vendors are marketing products around "network-based" security, where devices on the network monitor the presence of unauthorized devices or activities. "Network-based" means that these devices service both device and the network as a whole, as opposed to server-based security like firewalls or anti-virus that focus on information arriving and leaving the host-cum-bastion device. These products are sometimes called Intrusion Prevention Services (IPS) but in fact might be closer to Intrusion Detection Services (IDS). The capabilities of network-based security will vary from vendor to vendor, but will likely include the ability to detect newly arrived devices through MAC address checks and the correlation of a traffic profile against known MACs. In this way they can alert administrators to potential security incidents.

Response: Safeguards Around End-Point Device Risks.

10. *Security Event Management (SEM)* Systems and Services. SEM services can provide vital information about the source of

threats to the converged network and statistics important to prioritizing and organizing responses.

11. *Network-Based Security.* Depending on the vendor, network-based security should also include the ability to isolate suspect devices on the network through on-the-fly switching/routing configuration changes that deny traffic from the device, ideally right at the LAN switch.

12. *See Operational Safeguards such as CIRT Services.*

Recovery: Safeguards Around End-Point Device Risks.
   See Operational Safeguards, Such as CIRT Services.

Prevent, detect, respond, and recovery are the four elements around which protocol, stacks, and architectural safeguards can be planned. The safeguards that have been recommended are presented below.

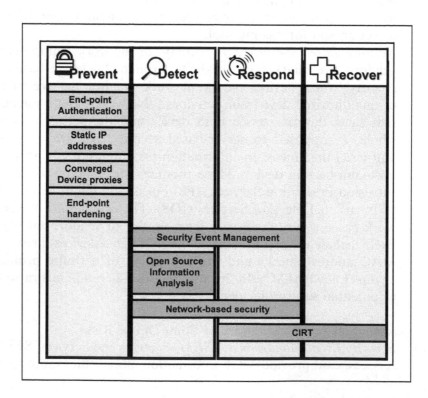

Asset			Recommendations		
	Threat Assessment	Risk Assessment	Proposed Controls and Safeguards	Residual Risks	Assessment of Safeguards
Data	9	Low	• End-point authentication • Static IP addresses • Converged device proxies • End-point hardening • SEM • Open source security information • Network-based security • CIRT	Low	Completely satisfactory
VOIP	9	High		Medium	Needs improvement; impacts on latency still very uncertain if safeguards applied
Entertainment and Media	9	High		High	Needs improvement; impacts on latency still very uncertain if safeguards applied; digital rights enforcement very uncertain
Physical	9	High		Low	Completely satisfactory
SCADA	9	High		Low	Satisfactory in most aspects
Banking	9	Low		Low	Satisfactory in most aspects
Facilities	9	High		Low	Completely satisfactory
Metering	9	High		Low	Satisfactory in most aspects

CONCLUSION

Despite the number of controls and safeguards discussed in this chapter, there remains a significant number of assets in every threat class with the assessment of residual risk rated as "Needs Improvement." This reflects the fact that there are assurance issues to be addressed around ICT convergence in the future. Some of the solutions will be management oriented; some will be operationally oriented; and others will be technical. The next two chapters will discuss how to effectively manage and operate contemporary controls and safeguards for ICT networks and what we might see in the future.

A final point to be made about this chapter regarding the risks which "Need Improvement": managers should recall (from Chapter 2) that there are three ways to deal with risks. First, risks can be accepted and businesses will continue to operate as usual, with the assumption being that the vulnerability will not be exploited (odds too low), or that the damage inflicted will be recoverable with less cost than the proposed controls and safeguards. Second, managers can apply more controls and safeguards but only if these controls and safeguards are available. Third, risks can be transferred to third parties through vehicles like insurance, supplier agreements, and even client-contract terms and warranties.

5

Managing Assurance

AUTHOR: **Tyson Macaulay**
Bell Security Solutions, Inc.

- **INTRODUCTION**
- **TARGET AUDIENCE**
  Regulatory Assurance Checklists (RAC)
  Security Metrics and ICT Management
- **RATE IMPLEMENTATION AND TESTING REGIME FOR CONVERGED NETWORKS**
- **IMPACT ASSESSMENT CHECKLIST**
- **CONCLUSION**

INTRODUCTION

> *A friendly reminder*: The objective of this book is not to provide a fundamental course on ICT security management. Our intent is to document some new techniques for managing the evolving assurance requirements of converged IP networks. Virtually everything that is applicable around the good management of contemporary data-only networks is still applicable to the security of converged IP networks. This chapter represents some of the change, the "delta," between data-only network security and converged network security.

In Chapter 2 entitled Enterprise Risk Management, we discussed the use of metrics in managing converged networks. In this chapter we will expand on this discussion by introducing some of the latest techniques involving security metrics to the management of converged ICT systems.

In Chapter 4: Controls and Safeguards, we mentioned two specific management safeguards to support the maintenance of assurance of converged network:

- Regulatory Assurance Checklists (RAC)
- Information Assurance Checklists (IAC).

Both of these concepts represent expanded thinking in the area of ICT security and will be further developed and demonstrated in this chapter. Also in Chapter 4, we mentioned the use of Readiness and Testing Environments (RATE) as a Prevention and Detection safeguard without a detailed explanation of how a RATE might be established. RATEs are not new; they are common safeguards in many organizations dealing with high-assurance requirements for data and information such as financial institutions and government entities. But relative to the population of businesses that will soon be dependant on converged ICT assets, the use of RATE is minuscule. The upshot is that the use of RATE controls and safeguards in the management of ICT assets will become a requirement across a much broader range of organizations in the near future. For this reason it is worth reviewing RATE tools and methodologies at a high level, so that these tools and methodologies can become more accessible.

TARGET AUDIENCE

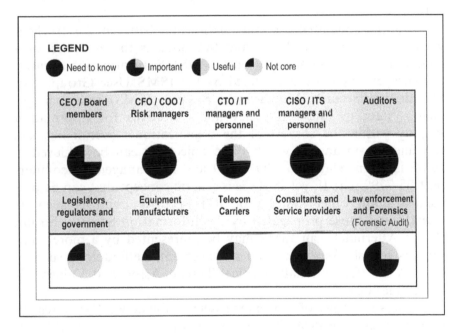

These days no book about ICT security would be complete without mention of ISO 17799: the International Standard Organization's (ISO) Code of Practice for Information Security Management, the juggernaut of ICT security methodologies. The most important thing to know about ISO 17799 in the context of this book, and convergence in general, is that it supplies an excellent starting point for management, operational, and technical controls around generic ICT security. However, ISO 17799 was developed with Data-oriented controls and safeguards and did not take into account converged sensitivity. For this reason it falls under the category of "what is" as opposed to the delta or "what has changed" concerning ICT convergence and the assurance of converged assets on IP networks.

Another potentially useful relationship between the excellent work surrounding ISO 17799 and this book is the evolution of a concept known in the security world as ISMS: Information Security Management Systems. As defined by the ISMS User Group: "An Information Security Management System (ISMS) is a management system to establish policy and objectives for information security within the context of the organization's overall business risk and the means by which these objectives can be achieved."[1] ISMS is often related to ISO 17799 and its management counterpart BS 7799 part II, yet ISMS is a generic concept that can be predicated upon other systems of ICT security controls such as CoBIT[2] and those propagated by the Information Security Forum (ISF).[3] Alternately, an ISMS may be represented by a more comprehensive risk assessment and management methodology such as OCTAVE,® (Operationally Critical Threat, Asset, and Vulnerability Evaluation).[4]

The appearance of converged assets on the network is no reason to junk an existing ISMS if one is already in place. If an ISMS is in place, convergence would necessitate a review of the controls and safeguards based upon the information contained in the pervious chapters about new or emerging threats, risks, and safeguards. The management techniques covered in the remainder of this chapter

---

[1] http://www.xisec.com/faqs.htm.

[2] http://www.isaca.org.

[3] http://www.securityforum.org.

[4] http://www.cert.org/octave.

represents components of an ISMS that managers should consider as adjuncts to the tools and methodologies that they chose to adopt. Some of the tools described will resemble variations on existing systems of asset management and assessment, tweaked to apply to convergent technologies.

Regulatory Assurance Checklists (RAC)

Regulatory requirements (national, state, or municipal statutes and regulations to which an organization must comply) are now a potent driver of ICT security and assurance requirements. The current crop of applicable statutes is represented by examples such as Sorbanes Oxley, Graham Leach Blighy, and ubiquitous Privacy legislation. The names may change over the coming years, but it is highly unlikely that ICT assurance will become any less regulated than it is currently. Regulatory requirements will merely be better defined in the future.

In Chapters 3 and 4 we traced some new threats and risks around convergence, which have emerged as a result of new legislation and regulations, and the potential safeguards that might be considered. One of the safeguards mentioned is possibly an innovation of this book; specifically, the Regulatory Assurance Checklist (RAC).

A RAC does not need to be a complex document; simple is better. The audience for a RAC will be anyone concerned with regulatory (business) requirements and how they impact technical and operational requirements. In effect, a RAC will define the top-level management issues for an organization. The requirements will be re-usable across the organization for all systems design and architecture exercises. A well-executed systems design methodology should start with the gathering of regulatory requirements as the first step, then successively drill down to deeper and deeper business, technical, and design layers. Each layer should be derived and mapped back to the layer above it, so that in the end, every technical feature of a system, application, or process is traceable back to either an explicit regulatory requirement or a formally expressed management requirement (such as an approved organizational policy). And every set of security requirements should include a comprehensive list of regulatory requirements. The following

diagram is a simplistic display of how an RAC would fit into a system design methodology.

This methodology is not new. In fact, it is a simple expression
of tried and true systems engineering processes. The advantage of
deploying these processes in managing the assurance of converged
networks and assets is that no business requirement is left unad-
dressed in deployment, and no "do-overs" need occur. Do-overs
tend to be very expensive when the business requirement is not a matter of regulatory requirement, but could be catastrophic in the event

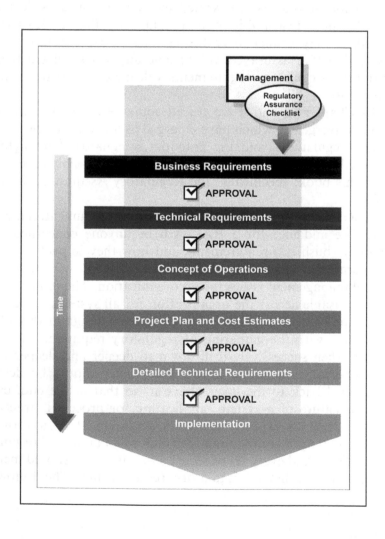

that the overlooked requirement was a regulatory requirement. For this reason, regulatory requirements need to be assessed, defined, and documented as an executive-level expression of business requirements that must enter into the design and implementation of all converged assets.

Ideally, the RAC will start with an outline of the statutes and regulations applicable to the organization. The determination of what is applicable to an organization is a matter for corporate legal council to determine in cooperation with regulators. Many businesses will be covered by one of the types of regulatory requirements covered in Chapter 3, but probably many more regulations at the state and municipal level of government as well. An additional consideration is what statutes and regulations apply to the systems and processes that are governed by a converged asset. Could the workplace become physically dangerous to employees if a particular asset on the network was compromised? For example, if fire detection systems are off-line. Health and Safety regulations may therefore impact the RAC for assets such as Physical Security and Facilities Management. As another example: If an asset compromise could result in the unauthorized release of toxic elements, Environmental Safety may play a role. For the most part, because ICT is so critical to all business processes, all significant statutes and regulations that govern an organization should be expressed in the RAC and their linkage to ICT defined in clearer terms.

Once these statutes and regulations have been identified, then they should be enumerated and annotated with the specific section and text of interest. For the most part, these involve sections of the statue or regulation relating to:

- Proscriptions around ICT safeguards such as information handling and reporting (à la SoX, GLB, Privacy legislation)
- Proscriptions around functional safety (i.e., Health and Safety and Environmental Safety) with the linkage being that many physical assets used in production may be controlled and monitored through ICT-dependant assets
- Sanctions associated with non-compliance

The following RAC format may prove useful:

Requirement number	Statute name	Information handling	Functional safety	Sanctions
1	Gramm-Leach-Bliley[5] (Financial Modernization Act of 1999)	Secure management of information	NA	Fines, director liability
2	Gramm-Leach-Bliley (Financial Modernization Act of 1999)	Protection of personal information	NA	Fines, director liability
3	Environmental Health and Safety	Emergency response procedures must be available to all staff	Workers must not be exposed to hazardous substances (the control and monitoring of which is managed by a converged asset)	Fines, director liability

The result of this exercise will be the regulatory requirements for converged assets. Most managers will be surprised by the amount of regulatory requirements that are potentially impacted. by convergence! Many will possibly reject the RAC assessment exercise because they have been operating without this information successfully (blissfully) "for years." While this may be true, no one has been operating under converged ICT assets for very long. The emergence of converged sensitivity makes these management tools extremely important in understanding the changing regulatory risks facing organizations.

Regulatory requirements should be related to different converged asset categories (data, voice, physical security, etc.), and perhaps at specific assets at lower levels, as required (for instance, within Physical Security: CCTV, door strikes, motion detectors). From these requirements, existing safeguards should be mapped in a matrix on a one-to-many (requirement-to-safeguard) basis so that no requirement is overlooked and with safeguards grouped as management, operational, or technical. It is possible that many safeguards will be generated by a single requirement; however, it is also likely that many

---

[5] http://www.ftc.gov/privacy/glbact/glbsub1.htm.

safeguards will be common across all requirements. Finally, a RAC is not intended to document only new safeguards for converged assets—they should document the entire range of ICT safeguards employed by an organization. The following table is an example of mapping regulatory requirements to existing safeguards.

It is possible that this exercise will require a significant time investment initially, but once the regulatory requirements and safeguards have been documented once, annual maintenance will require substantially less effort.

The final element of the RAC is to define and assign ownership of the safeguards in the form of an actual checklist: Who owns the accountability for the safeguards? Is the safeguard implemented and up-to-date? The best way to approach this will vary from organization to organization. In most cases it may not make sense to organize safeguard-ownership around a converged asset because many of the safeguards will be common across multiple assets, just as threats are common across multiple assets. In this instance the solution is likely based upon existing structures, with top management (CIO-type entity) owning all Management safeguards, and asset owners (possibly many owners inside some classes of asset, such as Data with its many

Asset: Data			
Requirement number	Management safeguards	Operational safeguards	Technical safeguards
1	• Top tier ISP • Supplier management • Outsourced disaster site • Enterprise risk management	• Application of ISO 17799	• Firewalls • IDS • Data encryption
2	• Log management policies • Enterprise risk management	• Log management procedures • Application of ISO 17799	• Access controls on logs • Data encryption
3	• Training and awareness policy • Yearly update cycle on procedures • Table-top emergency exercises	• Redundant location for access to emergency procedures • Hardcopies available in marked locations • Application of 17799 controls	• Firewall between Data network and SCADA network • IDS on SCADA network

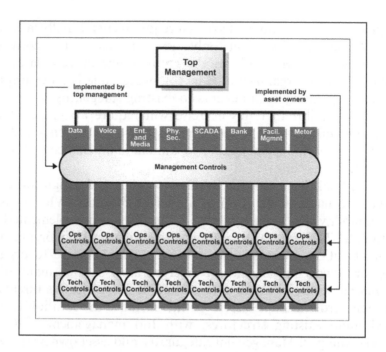

distinct systems, applications, and processes) owning all Technical and Operational safeguards.

Once a RAC has been implemented and an organization has some insight into what it needs to be compliant from a regulatory perspective, it is a matter of how to measure, monitor, and manage compliance.

Security Metrics and ICT Management

The more assets converge on the IP network, the more important ICT security metrics become to an organization. Metrics are a key part of a well-designed and managed ISMS (Information Security Management System), which can re-introduce order into an increasingly challenging security environment.

> An especially challenging security environment is created when new technologies are deployed. Risks often are not fully understood, administrators are not yet experienced with the new technology, and security controls and policies must be updated. Therefore, agencies should carefully

consider such issues as: their level of knowledge and training in the technology, the maturity and quality of their security practices, controls, policies, and architectures, and their understanding of the associated security risks.[6]

This is a discussion about where to start with security metrics since this is the stage in which most organizations find themselves. For this reason we will focus on the simpler and more popular systems of metrics that are available. Drawing from the material covered in Chapter 2: Enterprise Risk Management, the reader will recall that metrics come in two flavors, qualitative and quantitative. Qualitative metrics are the simplest forms of metrics to collect and manage; their current popularity is testament to this fact. Quantitative metrics can also be very simple as we will see, but essentially have no limit in the complexity. They also tend to produce results that are traceable back to a fact, while qualitative metrics tends to trace back to an opinion.

Qualitative Metrics Systems

If we are to discuss ICT security and qualitative metrics, we should discuss "maturity" models. "Maturity models" is an engineering term adopted into the security vernacular to express the level of discipline, effectiveness, and completeness found in an organization's systems of managing ICT security. As we are about to see, there are a variety of different maturity models to choose from, but many of them tend toward recognizably similar definitions of maturity level... which is a good thing, at least for comparing security metrics between organizations using distinct methodologies. However, be warned that several organizations, associations, consultancies, and miscellaneous entities have latched on to the term "maturity model" or "maturity level" and have created/published metrics methodologies that are very parochial. These models often have one single thing in common with the major maturity models discussed here—they tend to have five levels. Other than that, they are purpose-built and generally not very meaningful outside that purpose. For instance, some governments have created a variety of qualitative metrics tools based upon highly parochial maturity models to measure policy

---

[6] NIST 800-58, Security Consideration for VOIP systems, pg 6.

compliance. It is as important to know both the maturity model that was applied as it is the maturity metric/level that is being reported.

As with many security and technology innovations, maturity models were derived from U.S. military research. The U.S. Department of Defense engaged Carnegie Mellon University to establish the Software Engineering Institute (SEI) to support the development of applications with military-grade reliability and validity. The Capability Maturity Model for Software (CMM-SW) was first published by SEI in 1991 and various other models since then, culminating ultimately in the release of the Capability Maturity Model Integration (CMMI) framework in 2002. The Information Systems Audit and Controls Association published its CoBit (Control Objectives of Information and related Technology) model in 1996 (revised twice since) with five maturity levels. The CMM model was also extended specifically into security engineering with the publication of ISO 21827: Security Systems Engineering-Capability Maturity Model (SSE-CMM) in 2002. To complete the sweep for the concept of maturity models in the management of ICT systems and security, the National Institute of Standards and Technology published NIST 800-55: Security Metrics Guide with its five "levels of effectiveness" in 2003. The following table summarizes these three qualitative techniques around ICT security derived from the original SEI work.

Maturity model	Maturity levels
CoBIT	1. Initial/ad hoc 2. Repeatable but intuitive 3. Defined processes 4. Managed and measurable 5. Optimized within business
SSE-CMM	1. Performed informally 2. Planned and tracked 3. Well-defined 4. Quantitatively controlled 5. Continuously improving
NIST 800-55	1. Policy statements signed off 2. Procedures developed according to policy 3. Implementation across the entire organization 4. Testing of controls 5. Integration with business processes

Note: While these techniques and methodologies may, in some instances, consider themselves to be "quantitative" because they attempt to derive maturity level values from percentages, averages, and other apparently empirical data, the means by which these data are collected renders them more qualitative than quantitative in the opinion of the author. The reason for this assessment is that while all the information requested by these methodologies could be collected empirically, in practice it is not. It is collected through interviews with people and often the very people responsible for the secure operation of a given asset. In most cases people will answer in ad hoc fashion and provide answers that are least likely to get them into trouble with management; this makes the answers "opinion" more than quantifiable fact. That is human nature. Another factor related to the distinction of these models as qualitative is that they tend to include the availability and use of quantitative metrics as an indicator of the highest form of maturity, Level 5. Following this reasoning, it might be argued that these methodologies are, in fact, qualitative until they are employed by a Maturity Level 5 organization.

Maturity models have played a significant part in the advancement of ICT security management practices and provided the first generation of popularized and widely accepted metrics that can be used for dashboard-type applications. Maturity models were successful probably because they placed an emphasis on simplicity and comprehension and represented "something" where nothing had really existed before.

Maturity models continue to gain in popularity but, as discussed earlier, their simplicity lends them to adoption for highly specific and esoteric purposes. The result is that the concept of maturity level is becoming very confused despite the emergence of some real champions like CoBIT, SSE-CMM, and NIST 800-55. Possibly as a reaction to this, models for true quantitative metrics are being increasingly discussed and are in fact going through ISO standards processes.

Quantitative Metrics Systems

We mentioned at the start of this chapter that ISO 17799 was the juggernaut of ICT security methodologies. Not only is this true, but it is also attracting some of the most advanced thinking around ICT security and assurance, and has naturally spawned an effort around metrics. The metrics being proposed as a complement to ISO 17799 are quantitative metrics, perhaps reflecting the post-maturity model generation of ICT security metrics. Opinions about the impending ascendancy of quantitative metrics will vary, if for only one reason: They are difficult and expensive to gather relative to qualitative metrics.

The ISO ICT security metrics are currently under development at the time of this writing with a working title of ISO 27004, and resemble a duality of metrics which should be applied under the standard:

- Progress metrics, which show improvement over time
- Performance metrics, which show effectiveness of controls/safeguards at a given time

Progress metrics might monitor the number of controls that have been completely satisfied from one of the detailed (and complex) security methodologies we have already mentioned: ISO 17799, ISF, NIST 800-26, OCTAVE, CoBIT, SSE-CMM, etc. All these methodologies have dozens of controls in different categories, and most organizations will fulfill only a handful initially. So it becomes possible to track which controls an organization has successfully applied over time to come out with a very simple quantitative metric. An example of this type of quantitative metric based upon ISO 17799 was proposed even in advance of ISO 27004.[7]

Progress metrics possibly represent the lowest hanging fruit on the quantitative metrics tree. They are relatively simple to understand and manage, and because they can be implemented using well developed frameworks like ISO, they can be easily employed in comparisons across organizations because multiple organizations can agree on the legitimacy of these "standards."

The downside of progress metrics is that underlying them may be the same sort of human-centric interview and audit procedures that underlie the maturity-level metric systems, and has resulted in them being "down-graded" in this book to the status of qualitative metrics. (Acknowledged these are harsh words for excellent work.) If progress metrics associated with international standards are to push beyond what has been accomplished with

---

[7] David A. Chapin, *How can security be measured?*, Information Systems Control Journal, Volume 2, 2005, ISACA.

maturity levels, they will need to be supported by valid and reliable processes for assessing compliance and non-compliance with controls. The resulting assessments must support clear, binary judgments of what is "compliant" or "non-compliant." Further to the point: Any implementation of progress metrics must display an ability to revoke compliance opinions as well as grant them, and should do so without hesitation. In other words, progress can be up or down and the techniques must have no bias as to which direction an organization moves.

Performance metrics are the other side of the ISO 27004 metrics coin. They involve the gathering of data that have been tuned to ISO 17799 controls. The standard will not define specifically what these metrics should be or how they will be collected. The concept is that each control an organization wishes to apply will be mapped to a performance metric that makes sense in the context of the control. Clearly this methodology for generating ICT security metrics is not limited to ISO 17799 in its application.

In simplistic terms, quantitative metrics will be developed using one of four different scales. An understanding of these scales is useful to understanding how to approach the association of metrics with security controls:

- *Nominal*—The measurement values are grouped by type but are otherwise arbitrary. For example, the classification of intrusion attempts by their technique, such as Trojan or Buffer Overflow, but does not imply order among the categories.
- *Ordinal*—The measurement values are in an incremental ordering. For example, the assignment of different attack-types according to a system of severity levels.
- *Interval*—Measurement by frequency. For example, how often a virus successfully penetrates perimeter security (due to unauthorized entry points into the network).
- *Ratio*—The measurement of one quantitative value relative to another quantitative value. For example, if there are five recommended features within a given control, what numbers are implemented relative to the total?

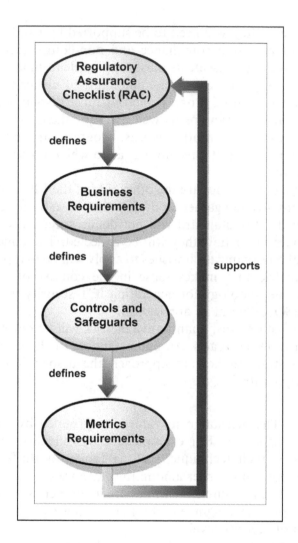

Choosing Quantitative Metrics: The choice of which metrics an organization should utilize in its ISMS will have been defined by the business requirements for the converged assets, as defined in the Regulatory Assurance Checklist previously described.

In this manner, the effort and resources required to generate quantitative metrics can be directly tied back to business justifications. Metrics chosen for their convenience or ease of use may have only tenuous linkages back to the business requirements. The table below offers an example of how to map the selection of metrics to business requirements.

Business requirement	Control	Metric	Type
Gramm-Leach-Bliley[8] (Financial Modernization Act of 1999): Secure management of information	ISO 17799 Control 10.3.2: Encryption	What proportion of data stores is protected by encryption from unauthorized access?	Percentage
	ISO 17799 Control 4.3.1: Security Requirements in outsourced contracts	N of the 7 recommended contract elements are present in supplier contracts	Ratio
Environmental Health and Safety: Emergency response procedures must be available to all staff	ISO 17799 Control 8.1.3: Incident management procedures	N of the 16 recommended contract elements are present in response procedures	Ratio

It would be highly premature to announce the demise of Maturity Models in ICT security management. No one is saying that Maturity Models are defunct and/or inadequate to preserve assurance of converged networks. Qualitative metrics require more expertise and resources to implement, understand, and maintain. Organizations undergoing convergence of their assets onto IP platforms without the benefit of a metrics methodology should start with qualitative Maturity Models as a first step. Get used to and learn to use qualitative metrics; then upgrade to the simpler forms of quantitative metrics discussed here.

RATE IMPLEMENTATION AND TESTING REGIME FOR CONVERGED NETWORKS

As mentioned previously, RATE stands for Readiness and Testing Environment and is a well-known safeguard in high-assurance data environments, especially environments such as Financial services where high availability is a major requirement.

---

[8] http://www.ftc.gov/privacy/glbact/glbsub1.htm.

This section will attempt to describe modifications to RATE systems that organizations should consider adopting as a fundamental safeguard for their converged assets and to preserve assurance on the converged networks.

A typical RATE system will emulate the operational infrastructure, including the same operating systems, software versions, and patch levels. The RATE system will also normally include identical hardware or sometimes smaller models of operational hardware (as long as the processor, disks, and memory architecture are the same). The purpose of a RATE methodology is to validate functionality (i.e., the system does what it is supposed to do) and check reliability (i.e., the system performs predictably) after a change has occurred (patch or upgrade, for instance) through the following types of tests:

1. Functionality test looking for bugs
2. Load tests
3. Input integrity tests (what happens if badly formatted or illegitimate data are loaded)
4. Output integrity tests (by loading rate system output into programs which simulate upstream/down stream processing)
5. Disaster recovery and fail over
6. Penetration tests against applications and operating system platforms
7. Network environmental impact testing (how network traffic might change)

While RATE systems are part of best practice around the assurance of any type of network, system, service, or application, it is usually reserved for large and important applications. Converged sensitivity requires that RATE processes be extended, not to merely large and important systems or services, but to just about all additions to the converged network, whether servers, network devices, or end-points. This is not to advocate that a full RATE regime be exercised against each and every device. The objective is to understand what the converged device is really doing to the network through a process of exposure and observation in a simulated environment. This is especially useful for devices that have recently converged onto IP and are therefore especially unpredictable in their behavior and design. We are referring to a "lite" RATE environment, which at minimum can support two of the seven tests mentioned previously: penetration tests and network environmental impact testing (how network traffic might change).

Using this "lite" RATE environment, all new devices (phones, meters, video cameras, etc.) should first undergo a series of penetration tests to determine to what extent they may be vulnerable to compromise and attack given the threats discussed in Chapters 3 and 4 concerning Green protocols, stacks and architectures and End-point security. Penetration tests can be conducted in a wide number of ways using commercial or public domain tools. Generally, the effectiveness of a penetration test is determined by the operators as opposed to the tools available, so engage good people for the testing and establish a process for documenting and assessing the results of the RATE testing.

Network environmental impact testing is carried out through observation and analysis both in parallel and distinctly from penetration testing in the RATE environment. This means that the device should be observed under stress (during the penetration tests = "abnormal operating conditions") and under "normal" operating conditions. Additionally, network environmental impact testing should be conducted both in a "sterile" network environments and in a simulated "live" network environment. A sterile environment is one where the only traffic is that related to the device(s) being tested and the test equipment; a simulated live environment would involve filling the RATE network with traffic which is as similar as possible to the intended environment in which the device will eventually reside.

The objectives of these environmental impact tests are defined in the following table.

The prescriptions above imply a capability that is normally outside the scope and functionality of most RATE environments—simulation of traffic. Simulation of traffic can be extremely problematic because it would be very expensive and difficult to attach a sample of every device in a converged network to a RATE network, and then get it "acting" like itself under normal operation. The solution is the employment of either network diodes or network taps or both in order to fill the RATE network with data traffic.

A network diode is a device that allows traffic to pass in one direction but not the other. These diodes can be configured to only allow certain types of information or volumes of information through to the RATE network on the other side. Network diodes are commercially available devices that have a variety of security applications, with RATE network simulation being in example. Diodes may very well support routable interfaces on both networks for purposes such as administration. A network tap is a simpler device, which simply sits on a network in "monitor" or "promiscuous" mode and makes a copy

	Sterile environment	Simulated environment
Normal operation	Unexpected/unexplained traffic emissions related to: ■ Malicious code or back doors ■ Faulty code ■ Unauthorized or unexpected license management functions ■ Undocumented features/services	Unexpected/unexplained traffic emissions related to: ■ Network loads and QoS impacts ■ Reactions to traffic loads ■ Reactions to errors or legitimate packets generated by other converged devices ■ Impact on IDS or IPS services
Stressed device	Unexpected reactions to stress: ■ Unexpected release of data ■ Broadcasting storms of errors (symptoms of a device having a "nervous breakdown") ■ Undocumented features or services that activate as reactions after certain types of attacks; for instance, to crafted packets	Unexpected reactions to stress and simulated traffic: ■ Network loads and QoS impacts ■ Reactions to traffic loads ■ Reactions to errors or legitimate packets generated by other converged devices ■ Impact on IDS or IPS services ■ Unexpected release of data ■ Broadcasting storms of errors (symptoms of a device having a "nervous breakdown") ■ Undocumented features or services which activate as reactions after certain types of attacks; for instance, to crafted packets

of all the network traffic, possibly right down to the ethernet frames. Unlike a diode, a tap will not send any information out into the network it is tapping and is therefore very difficult to detect because it is benign. In either case, traffic can be replicated from the intended live network environment to the RATE environment in order to simulate that environment for test purposes.

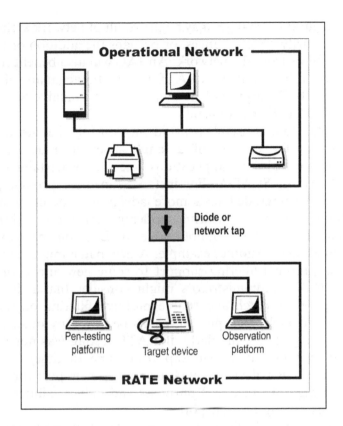

IMPACT ASSESSMENT CHECKLIST

An Impact Assessment Checklist (IAC) is a tool used to understand the impact of device-specific configuration changes on the full range of converged assets.

An IAC would likely be maintained for all interfaces of all major, configurable network modes, especially perimeter devices, and should document:

- The converged applications on the network (segment)
- The converged applications traversing the device
- The ports in use across all devices and applications
- The protocols in use on the given ports
- The QoS requirements of the given ports
- Rule sets
- Routing tables

Configuration changes may be the result of network architecture changes, security policy changes, or perhaps the addition or removal of devices to or from the network. An IAC will also benefit from the availability of the results from RATE testing. In fact, many of the elements of an IAC suggested below may not be available without the benefit of a RATE environment.

An IAC tool is useful to avoid introducing changes that may be benign in the context of a single asset such as Data, but pernicious to real-time applications such as Entertainment and Media, Voice, or SCADA. For instance, an older proxy-type firewall might be upgraded to a more advanced stateful or application-filtering firewall, which suddenly introduces 50 ms of additional latency; this is unnoticeable for Data but probably fatal to real-time assets. Another example: A new patch might be released expanding protocol filtering support to some new applications, for instance, H.323. Administrators might consider that it is a good step to apply the patch and enable protocol filtering on the given port. Unfortunately, that port may also be in use by other applications not using H.323. Similarly, if RATE testing was not undertaken (and let's face it, it will slip from time to time), it is very possible that a new device may be using a specific port for undocumented (benign or otherwise) purposes and induce failures in other applications relying on that port.

An IAC would be linked to an up-to-date network topology and be stored and maintained on the same basis as this topology.

To what extent are IACs practical given the work loads of a most network engineers/administrators/technicians and their known panache for paperwork and documentation? Probably not that practical, unless the concept of converged sensitivity is understood within an organization. Therefore, implementation of ISMS tools like IACs are really only practical when coupled with the Enterprise Risk Management practices discussed in Chapter 2, which expose the real risks associated with ad hoc network management practices in combination with converged networks. Chapter 6: What Comes Next? will offer some insight in alternatives to IACs which have been proposed.

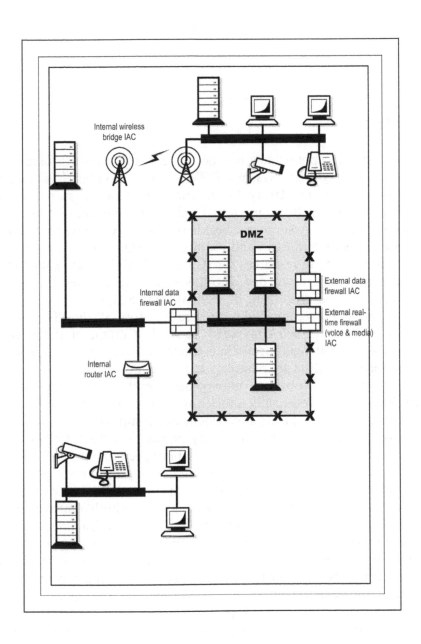

CONCLUSION

This chapter has presented a number of tools to support Information Security Management Systems (ISMS) for converged ICT assets: security metrics, regulatory tools, and configuration management tools in the form of Readiness and Testing Environment (RATE) systems and Impact Assurance Checklists (IAC). All these tools have costs associated with them and require both skill and time to implement, translating to resources for ICT security, which are sometimes difficult to justify (as anyone who has ever tried to develop a model for the return-on-investment of security can testify).

There is no recommendation here to adopt all the ISMS tools discussed to support a converged network. Certain of these tools represent lower-hanging fruit than others. For instance, Regulatory Assurance Checklists are relatively easy to compile and possess some very potent and obvious management-level information about requirements and especially sanctions. The cost of noncompliance is often sufficient to justify investment but compliance does necessarily contribute to production of any goods or service. Compliance reduces risks around issues such as liability, reputation, and cost of capital; it does not improve the bottom line, it prevents one potential source of erosion of the bottom line. It is the more complex tools discussed in this chapter that posses the ability to both improve assurance and demonstrate a contribution to the bottom line, namely security metrics and particularly quantitative metrics. The ability to generate accurate security metrics will demonstrate both evidence of requirements for security and very likely how greater security will drive greater efficiency and remove waste from the system. As an example, metrics around the type and duration of Voice sessions (just be careful of privacy issues!) might reveal abuse and misuse that, once addressed with appropriate policies and technical controls, might increase productivity and reduce costs associated with network upgrades (you don't need more switches and bandwidth right away, just less inappropriate usage). A further example of good security metrics contributing to the bottom line might be the area of transaction processing: maxed out firewalls or network connections slow processing times, which result in higher failure rates, fewer transactions, and therefore fewer transaction processing fees!

What Comes Next?

AUTHOR: Tyson Macaulay
Bell Security Solutions, Inc.

CONTRIBUTING AUTHOR: Lee Wagner
InCode Wireless

INTRODUCTION

In this final chapter we retain our methodology of addressing the topic of converged sensitivity according to management, operational, and technical subject matter. The material covered in this chapter is derived largely from contemporary academic research or (possibly) original notions presented here for the first time.

TARGET AUDIENCE

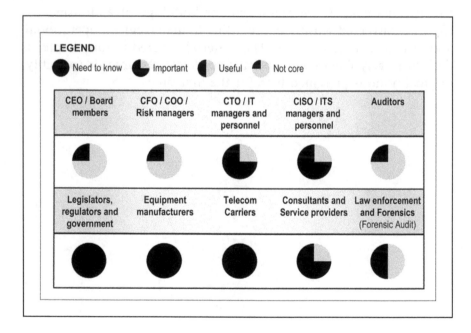

MANAGEMENT CONTROLS AND SAFEGUARDS

Internationally Relevant Compliance Requirements

The most pertinent developments and changes concerning the assurance requirements of converged assets will certainly be in the area of regulation and convergence. This is a very serious matter for all players in the convergence game, whether they be equipment makers, service providers, users, or the regulators themselves. Legislation and regulation can have massive effects on the assurance of converged ICT assets because they can enforce requirements upon many players (e.g., service providers, equipment manufacturers, auditors), which enhance assurance and mitigate threats impacting converged sensitivity. Legislation and regulation can also have market-distorting affects that are counter to the interests of business and consumers alike but perhaps suit the purposes of government.

In earlier chapters we discussed the Data-related requirements of legislative acts such as Sarbanes–Oxley (SoX) and Graham–Leach–Blighley (GLB) and how they are driving many requirements around the assurance of converged networks and assets. We also discussed some of the emerging legal requirements around lawful access and how VOIP, the catalyst for current convergence drives, poses some unique challenges to lawful access, the solutions to which are not yet apparent. The net result of these and many other disparate legislative activities is that there is really no consistent framework around the regulatory requirements for the assurance of converging, IP-based assets or ICT generally.

A situation similar to the one concerning assurance and converged assets existed over 25 years ago in the area of Privacy; a gap between legislative and regulatory requirements and technology was identified with the rapid growth of computer databases of consumer data. In the late 70s, a framework was developed by the OECD in the form of 10 privacy principles in 1980.[1] The OECD is a consultative and slow moving entity, which took into account inputs from a wide variety of sources and perspectives and its Privacy Principles have come to reflect the de facto privacy framework around which most privacy legislation is now founded, if not explicitly then implicitly. The importance of this comparison is that the privacy principles were successful in being acceptable to

---

[1] http://www.oecd.org/document/18/
0,2340,en_2649_34255_1815186_1_1_1_1,00.html.

government, citizens, and business by being logical and reasonable without being proscriptive. The OECD processes seems to have enforced this "reasonableness" because it is a completely consensus-driven body whose components do not reach consensus easily.

Legislation and regulation in the area of ICT convergence and security requirements has no such long standing OECD framework upon which to draw. To date it has been largely ad hoc and reactionary (to corporate abuses and equities crashes) or, in the case of some proposed VOIP regulatory requirements, panic driven. Fortunately, an international organization called the International Chamber of Commerce (ICC) has taken up the task of developing a framework of "principles" upon which ICT regulations and compliance issues could be developed by sovereign jurisdictions.

While the ICC purports to work closely with the OECD, it lacks the legitimacy of the OECD when it comes to the development and support of principles upon which governance and legislation should be based; however, the ICC ICT principles serve as an excellent input into the develop of a internationally accepted framework for ICT compliance matters. The draft principles as of the writing of this book are as follows:[2]

Consistent	Governments should ensure consistency among information compliance requirements. Differences among information compliance requirements and laws should be objectively justified, and their impact on business assessed. Governments should ensure effective international cooperation to avoid unnecessary differences; i.e., consistency is important both on a national and an international level.
Technology neutral	Any information compliance requirements should be technology neutral and stated in terms of functional objectives, rather than in prescribing solutions. Stated objectives should follow internationally-accepted terminology with a defined meaning in the information technology sector.
Future-proof	Any information compliance requirements should be sufficiently generic to accommodate future changes in technology which will undoubtedly occur, but which cannot be fully anticipated.

(Continued)

---

[2] Task Force on Security and Authentication, Commission on E-Business, IT and Telecoms, International Chamber of Commerce, Paris, Sept. 2005.

Standards-informed but not standards-specific	Government agencies that plan to introduce information compliance requirements should seek business advice on commonly-used industry standards and reference frameworks, and should avoid mandating specific standards. Standards used in compliance requirements should be market-driven in an open process with participation from all affected industries.
Mindful of economic impact	Governments should be mindful of the cost and potential additional liabilities associated with implementing information compliance policies and practices and should analyze the economic and social impact of these measures in the pre-existing regulatory environment before imposing information compliance requirements.
Clear	Information compliance requirements and applicable sanctions for noncompliance should be expressed clearly and unambiguously.
Nondiscriminatory	Governments should avoid creating government-controlled, operated or dominated compliance infrastructures. If such infrastructures are required, information compliance requirements in laws should not favor their use over other available information compliance products, services or infrastructures.
Enforcement	Enforcement of information compliance requirements in law should be nondiscriminatory and allow reasonable time for businesses to remedy shortcomings once identified.
Flexible	Governments should recognize that private sector compliance may require different approaches depending on factors such as a company's sector(s) of activity, connectivity, geographic spread, size, as well as economic or strategic importance.
Pro-competitive	Compliance requirements should avoid creating competitive disadvantages within and across national and sectoral borders.
Pro-trade	Information compliance requirements in laws should not create or maintain obstacles to international trade, including the cross-border delivery and use of information compliance products and services. Specific national information compliance requirements and standards can cause entry barriers for foreign importers or services providers, which in addition to creating obstacles to trade can negatively affect the competitiveness of local businesses.
Resources and preparedness	Governments should ensure before creating information compliance requirements that information and support services are in place to respond to reasonable business questions about the requirements and their practical implications. Governments should also ensure that enforcement officers before information compliance requirements become effective have the training and means that are required to ensure effective, neutral and consistent enforcement, and that enforcement decisions are published in a timely manner.
Period of grace and independent appeal	Governments should offer companies a period in which any systems that are deemed to be non-compliant by regulatory authorities can remedy such shortcomings in order to avoid sanctions. Final compliance decisions by regulatory authorities should be appealable to an independent body with sufficient power and means to decide and effectively enforce decisions in a reasonable timeframe.

It would be nice if governments could have an consensus-based framework on ICT security compliance from someone like the OECD to build upon. Otherwise, we will end up with a patch-work of geographically-based micro-regulations concerning an ethereal asset—information. We are already seeing this with the converge approaches between Canada and the United States around VOIP regulation and lawful access requirements. Without an internationally relevant set of guidelines for ICT regulation and compliance, countries and jurisdictions will risk hobbeling local businesses relative to the same (competing) business across the border.

OPERATIONS CONTROLS AND SAFEGUARDS

Automation of Complex Impact Assessments

As networks become larger and more complex, the difficulty associated with managing architectures and security role-sets will increase. IP convergence will make this issue even more critical for two very simple reasons: 1) converged sensitivity has increased the value and therefore the risks associated with a compromise to network assurance, and 2) there will be many more devices on the same physical network. But what is so difficult about managing architectures and security role-sets in the first place?

Leaving aside issues around simple capacity management, access control is the largest challenge. "In a networked system many devices, such as routers, firewalls, virtual private network gateways, and individual host operating systems must cooperate to achieve security goals. These devices may require different configurations, depending on their purposes and network locations. To solve many information security problems, one needs models of these devices and their interactions."[3]

Unauthorized access can occur in a wide variety of forms such as unauthorized devices, hackers, malicious insiders, virus, worms, etc. Unauthorized access can result for many reasons: malicious and/or misguided insiders, software vulnerabilities, administrator error, poor password or credential management, to name a few. And what aggravates the situation most after unauthorized access is gained is that much of the network may become available from a single entry point. Therefore, a typical sort of network best practice is to segment the network into security zones and limit the traffic that transits these zones and contacts end-point devices to what is required within that zone or by that device. In theory, this is a simple enough task accomplished through good management of firewalls, routers, switches, and end-point devices. In reality, the size and complexity of most networks coupled with the dynamic natures of the devices and services being attacked, makes management of good security architecture extremely difficult and getting harder all the time.

Every time a new server is added and a firewall rule is changed, a new segment added, or the topology is updated, the impact ripples across the network. In many cases, the impact is not fully understood. For

---

[3] Joshua Guttman, Amy Herzog, *Rigorous Automated Network Security Management*, The MITRE Corporation, Aug. 2003.

instance, a new LAN segment is added in a building to support contractor workstations. This segment only allows the contractors access to the Internet through the DMZ where the public-facing servers reside. The firewalls between the DMZ and the Internet only allow connections on port 80 (WWW) from the Internet to the DMZ servers. These servers are hardened, well-maintained, and have never been compromised, but the servers and all the firewalls allow telnet access from addresses inside the DMZ for administrative purposes. The implication is that unknown enities on any Internet address have telnet access to the DMZ servers and firewalls! Suppose one of them gains access through password guessing? The point of this example is that human error around visualizing the effect of an architectural change resulted in a potentially serious impact on network assurance.

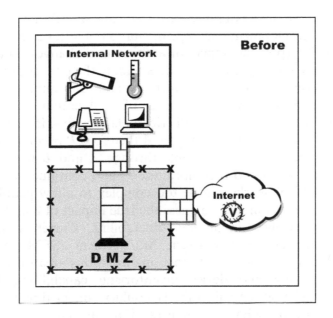

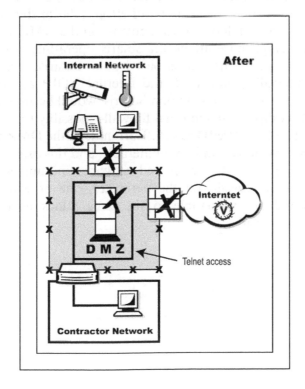

The increased assurance requirements of IP networks, will require the development and implementation of automated tools that can easily interpret the impact of architectural changes. These tools will be extremely important in understanding the impact of new software vulnerabilities to the network by allowing administrators to visualize the maximum potential reach of a vulnerability, based upon an exhaustive range of cause and effect relationships. If A is compromised due to a new vulnerability, and therefore B becomes an available target because it is available through A and B has the same vulnerability, assume B is compromised—and continue this process. Converged IP networks will be too complex to allow people, using nonexhaustive techniques, to guess the true impact of a architectural change or newly announced vulnerability. Currently available services such as Security Event Management (SEM) possess a complementary but low-level functionality in this area through their version tracking and device inventorying capabilities, but the estimation of how the vulnerability could result in threats to other assets is beyond SEM capabilities. For instance, the following diagram may display the cause-and-effect relationship between a contractor LAN with loose access controls on the DMZ, and a newly announced compromise attack on Solaris operating systems. Since the DMZ to internal firewall is based upon Solaris, it is impacted. Once the firewall is impacted, the internal VOIP phone systems, whose infrastructure is based upon Solaris, would become vulnerable through the compromised internal firewall—possibly to a new attack against the (compromised) firewall. Fortunately, the DMZ web server is based upon Windows and not vulnerable, and this organization has followed best practice for converged networks and implemented two distinct types of firewalls on the perimeter, one of which is Cisco IOS-based and not vulnerable to the same attack as the internal Solaris-based firewall.

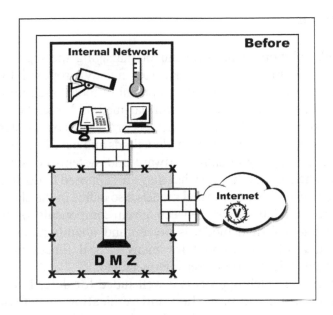

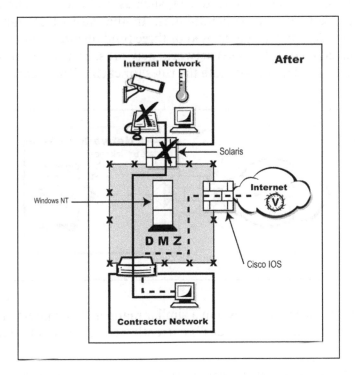

Formal Models

A possible solution to the problem of managing the highly complex security configuration of networks was initially proposed by Joshua Guttman in 1997[4] through the development of tools based upon formal methods and formal models. A "formal method" is embodied in an axiomatic process for describing artefacts or features of a system. "Formal models" are derived from formal methods and have long proven useful for developing high-quality software and systems considered both valid and efficient (i.e., they do what they are supposed to do and nothing more and they do it well). Formal models also define in the clearest terms the nature of relationships between given components of a system. Finally, while a formal model is precise and unambiguous, it is also abstract and will not account for many critical functional elements such as latency, loss, errors, user interfaces, etc.

A formal modeling process is well suited for describing network properties and for the simulation and verification of network behaviors when changes are introduced, such as architectural changes or the discovery of new vulnerabilities. In the case of IP networks, formal models may be comprised of three fundamental elements from the (converged or otherwise) network: networks, nodes, and end-point devices. Formal models denote the rules for each of these components

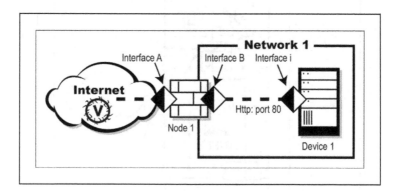

at the most basic policy level in a similar manner that routers and firewalls (both considered "nodes") currently record their rule sets.

---

[4] Joshua Guttman, *Filtering Postures: Local Enforcement for Global Policies*, In proceedings, 1997 IEEE Symposium on Security and Privacy, IEEE Computer Society Press, May 1997.

A very simple example of a formal model that described an architecture allowing only http traffic on port 80 to go from the Internet to the WWW server (device 1) would be represented by a rule set for each component in the network:

Network component	Interface	Source	Destination	Application
Node 1				
Allow	A	Any	Interface B	www: port 80
Deny	A	Any	Any	All
Allow	B	Interface	Device 1	www: port 80
Allow	B	Device 1	Interface	www: port 80
Deny	B	Any	Any	All
Network 1				
Allow		Node 1	Device 1	www: port 80
Allow		Device 1	Node 1	www: port 80
Deny		Any	Any	All
Device 1				
Allow	i	Node 1	Interface 1	www: port 80
Allow	i	Interface 1	Node 1	All
Deny	i	Any	Any	All

This example shows merely one external interface (*A*), one internal interface (*B*), one internal network and a single end-point device (WWW server). Obviously, even a mildly sophisticated organizational network would be represented by a far more complex model, and a converged network by an exponentially complex model! While this may seem horrendously complex and unwarranted, it is a fundamental representation of what network administrators often manage and track *intuitively*. The capturing and input of formal models will require significant effort initially (assuming the tools are available to manage these data), but once this information is inputted, it can be maintained and used as an exhaustive tool for managing assurance.

Converged IP networks need systems of formal modeling and tools that can support the input of relative simple changes and show the impacts of these changes across the network. These impacts will probably be categorized in two manners:

1. What unintended or unauthorized paths through the network have opened
2. What assets have been exposed

Furthermore, with formal models, it becomes possible to model the impact of a compromise in a network, mode, or device for unspecified reasons. What happens if an unprotected wireless LAN appears in the R&D section? What happens if a modem is connected to a desktop in accounting?

It would certainly be possible to couple these formal models with metrics, which would allow for a third dimension to the reporting: threat severity. Metrics such as the sensitivity of the assets being exposed and the completeness (i.e., are all IP cameras exposed? or just one?) of the exposure are two simple metrics that would support assessments of the threat.

TECHNICAL CONTROLS AND SAFEGUARDS

Overlay Networks

Overlay networks are not new concepts to the Data and IP world, and are represented in a simpler form by technologies such as Virtual Private Networks (VPNs). An overlay is a network within a network. However, overlay networks (ONs) are now being taken much further in research to try and account for a current failing of the Internet, namely resiliency. In the context of convergence, this is relevant because the techniques being developed for ONs related to resiliency also possess the capability to enhance assurance of IP-based assets, whether they be based upon the Internet of dedicated, purpose built IP networks such as financial transaction or industrial-control networks.

The names applied to the type of evolving ON about to be described are not standard and much of the excellent thinking in this area is in academic research. For this reason we will focus on the features of evolving ONs rather than what to call them. (For further information on overlay network, see David Andersen formerly of MIT and now Carnegie Mellon University.[5])

The first work around resilient ONs involved the development of gate-way proxy-type overlay routers that maintained information about the availability of different IP routes between a given gateway proxy and a destination.[5] The overlay router would encapsulate the data packets inside ON headers, which allows them to be routed according to instructions within the router that change according to network conditions. When a packet arrived for a given destination, the overlay router would first refer to an internal table about the health and speed of the different routes to a destination available from that point on the network/Internet, and would send the packet down the best route ("best" from the perspective of latency, loss, and error-rate). This reflected an innovation in regular IP routing through Border Gateway Protocol (BGP) which generally establishes a single favorite route between two points in the network and keeps this route intact unless something prolonged and serious occurs—by which point minutes may have passed.

---

[5] David Anderson, Hari Balakrishnan, Frans Kaashoek, Robert Morris, *Resilient Overlay Networks*, MIT 2001.

Diagram A below shows what might be a typical network path between a source and the destination of two independent ISPs, with the route reflecting the most expedient architecture for the ISP which must support many customers. Diagram B illustrates the potential impact of ONs on the efficient routing of traffic.

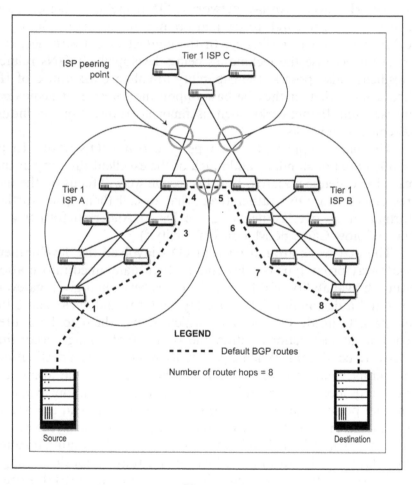

Diagram A

While this form of ON contributes to the moment to moment assurance of the IP network through reduced latency, loss, and errors, it also has the potential to specify and enforce which routes are used for different types of data based upon destination or even packet type. While BGP will eventually change the path information takes over a large network in response to prolonged outages, it may also inadvertently route information through hostile logical territory. ONs could be used to limit the available routes or simply exclude

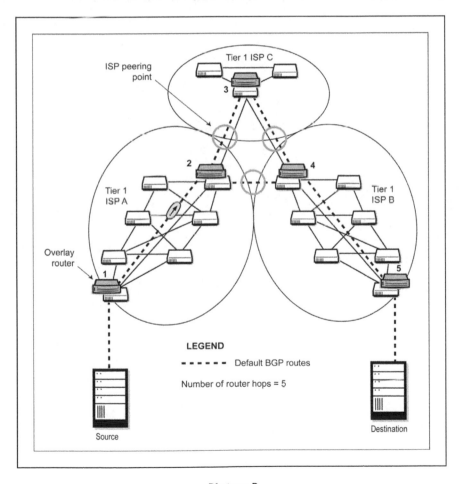

Diagram B

certain "unfortunate" routes from the list of alternates that might otherwise be available.

The impact of ONs on assurance could be substantial, especially in large corporate networks where certain types of asset traffic may be routed in a variety of ways, some of which are not acceptable from a security perspective. For instance, financial transactions from remote offices might take several paths through the organizational WAN in the event of a partial outage on the "usual" route; one of them should not be through the gigabit ethernet used by the VOIP-based call center, which is staffed by many casual, uncleared workers.

Multi-Path Overlays

Extending the notion of ONs is the addition of multi-homed networks. Mutli-homing is the connection of a given device or gateway router to two or more distinct outbound network connections. This means that data leaving the device or gateway has more than one way to leave. This type of access control is well known in the telecom world and is often implemented to as "double vault" access—two physically unique access points for telecom services into a building. In the case of IP networks, this translates into two distinct network interfaces supporting connections to two distinct ISPs. Multi-homing is also well used in technologies like Storage Area Networks (SANs) and high-availability systems where the foibles of a single network interface cannot satisfy availability requirements even on dedicated networks. (Even in the absence of any routing requirements on dedicated internal networks, hardware failures around network interfaces at the physical layer—the "wire"—may require multi-homing.)

One of the findings of Andersen et al.[6] regarding ONs was that while performance can be significantly increased and reactions to outages can be much faster than simply relying on the native control mechanism (BGP) on the Internet, there is still a 60% chance that if a packet fails to reach its destination (i.e., is lost) using default routing it will also fail using an ON. This reflects the realities of single-homed devices; i.e., that the failures are often so close to "home" that alternate routes on the open Internet will still encounter the same final blockage. ONs allow faster reactions to slow downs and improved performance, but they are greatly augmented/complemented by the addition of multi-homing on the devices or the routers. In this way, the ONs can monitor and direct traffic to destinations with a much greater certainty of improving the latency, loss, and error rates because multi-home mitigates failures at ISP choke-points along the way, such as peering points.[7]

---

[6] David Andersen, Alex C. Snoeren, Hari Balakrishnan, *Best-Path Versus Mutli-Path Overlay Routing*, MIT Labrattory for Computer Science, Oct. 2003.

[7] David Andersen, Hari Balakrishnan, M. Frans Kaashoek, Rohit N. Rao, *Improving Web Availability for Client with MONET*, Carnegie Mellon University, 2004.

Such Multi-path ONs represent another step toward the type of assurance required by converged networks, but do satisfy the full requirement by any standard. Even Multi-path ONs would not come close to meeting the latency, loss, and error rates that are required for many real-time and loss sensitive converged assets, as discussed in the previous chapters. Multi-path/multi-home capabilities are features that can be added at the same time as ONs or independently. This is an important point to keep in mind about this discussion; i.e., the safeguards and controls being discussed are not necessarily mutually dependant.

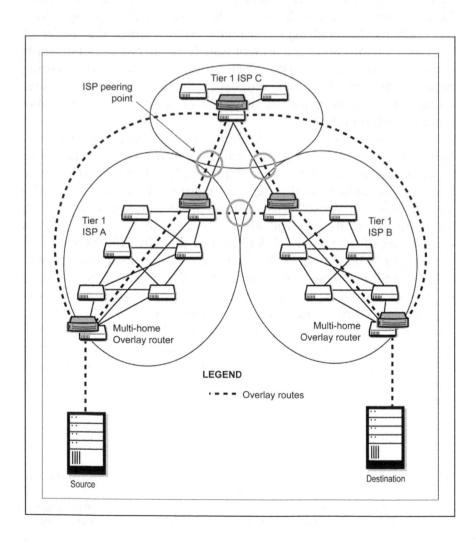

Multi-Homing with Inexpensive Network Connections (MINC)

A third, distinct but complementary network technology to ONs and mutli-path ONs is the concept of link striping. Link striping is not unlike the technique of disk striping, which involves the writing of data across 2 to 32 or more hard disks so that the failure of one disk will be compensated for automatically by the other disks and no information will be lost. Disk striping is also an important tool to improve input/output speed of data from disk storage devices. Disk striping is also known as RAID (Redundant Array of Inexpensive Disks). In the case of link striping, we are talking about multi-homing with inexpensive network connections (MINC).

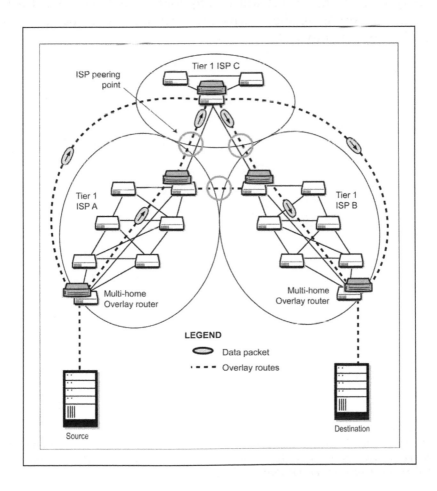

Some of the most recent work in the area of link striping has been done by Zhang et al.[8] and involves the modification of Transport Communications Protocol (TCP)– the linga franca of the Internet—to allow for data streams to be divided over different interfaces from a device or a proxy such that latency loss and error rates all improve. This result is accomplished through a variety of means building upon ONs, and fundamentally involves the direction of packets with the same destination down different routes; as one route reduces its performance, loads are shifted to the other available routes and interfaces.

This work concerning link striping is very valuable, but it still only reduces latency to seconds (as opposed to minutes for contemporary Internet best-path/BGP routing) and does not reflect the type of assurance that will be required for fully converged networks supporting multiple, sensitive, real-time assets based upon UDP as opposed to TCP.

---

[8] Ming Zhang, Junwen Lai, Arvind Krishnamurphy, Larry Peterson, Randolph Wang, *A Transport Layer Approach for Improving End-to-End Performance and Robustness Using Redundant Paths*, Princeton 2005.

Mixed Media Networks

A definition of convergence addressed earlier by this book was Fixed-Mobile Union (FMU): the combination of fixed line and wireless network technologies in such a way that ICT assets are unaware of what type of network link they are using. They automatically use the link with the best performance through the network protocol IMS (IP Multi-media Subsystem). FMU technologies can be applied to carry the evolution of network assurance further based on the business continuity advantages introduced by mixed media networks; i.e., networks constructed of a combination of fixed and mobile technologies with full redundant capabilities.

The business continuity advantages of FMU are numerous. FMU allows for support of strictly independent network ingress and egress points. This is important because it is often the case with so-called "redundant" network links that they occupy the same physical building access location, or the same right-of-way a few hundred meters down the road. Creating not one but many potential single points of fail for (not so) redundant fixed-line links. A wireless network always create a truly separate physical network at the point of access; this is an essential benefit for converged applications and networks critical to business. Wireless connections deployed in combination with fixed-line connections under FMU technologies create a stronger business continuity capability related to network availability than much more expensive all-fixed-line alternatives.

However, wireless connections possess some assurance questions especially concerning confidentiality of the asset's information. For instance, asset data that formally transversed only a fixed-wired physical infrastructure now also uses a wireless infrastructure. As a consequence, the ICT department has new security implications to consider related to the security of the wireless connections themselves. Can signals be intercepted? Yes, always; that is the nature of any wireless network. Can information be derived from intercepted signals? Again, yes; information related to traffic volumes and how they might correlate to other non-network observations will be available to skilled observers. Can data be read? Messages intercepted or inserted? For the most part, no, not if the wireless network is established properly. The topic of wireless security is a book unto itself, so we will not pursue this topic further other than to say that in most cases it can be made adequate for the purposes of secondary, business-continuity and network assurance purposes.

Generalized Environment for Network Investigations (GENI)

The National Science Foundation (NSF), ever on the cutting edge of Internet development, has recently announced a new project that appears to be very relevant to the topic of this book.

> The Directorate for Computer and Information Science and Engineering (CISE) is planning an initiative called Global Environment for Networking Investigations or GENI to explore new networking capabilities that will advance science and stimulate innovation and economic growth. The GENI Initiative responds to an urgent and important challenge of the 21st century to advance significantly the capabilities provided by networking and distributed system architectures.

> The GENI Initiative envisions the creation of new networking and distributed-system architectures that, for example:

> - Build in security and robustness;
> - Enable the vision of pervasive computing and bridge the gap between the physical and virtual worlds by including mobile, wireless and sensor networks;
> - Enable control and management of other critical infrastructures;
> - Include ease of operation and usability; and
> - Enable new classes of societal-level services and applications.[9]

More than that is not known at the time of this writing, but it would be reasonable to expect a great contribution to the assurance of converged IP network from GENI.

---

[9] http://www.nsf.gov/cise/geni.

CONCLUSION

This chapter has presented only a small snapshot of the potential innovations available concerning the development of ICT security and converged assets. The ideas in this chapter were not discussed or presented because they appear to be the most likely, short-term steps; rather, they were presented as some of the more thought-provoking innovations.

Will consensus-based ICT regulatory guidelines be established and gain weight and influence the way privacy principles did at the OECD 20-plus years ago? Hopefully. They are clearly required now. Will arcane and complex formal models for managing ICT networks be adopted? Perhaps not in an obvious, front-and-centre model, but the rigor and assurance that formal models support is clearly a major requirement for converged ICT networks. The rate of adoption of formal models is probably a matter of the development of a suitable interface to input and manage network configuration and topology information. Formal models are a matter of "when" and "how," not "if." Lastly, overlay networks and the mixing of network physical media: Overlay networks are a response to the unwillingness of Tier 1 ISPs to work together affect for legitimate competitive reasons. Overlays may never come to pass if appropriate peering relationships are established, yet overlays also possess interesting assurance properties related to the ability to route information dynamically and even predictably. Is this capability of possible interest to those concerned about high-resource and highly motivated threat agents? Probably.

This book has covered a lot of ground. Much of this ground is well understood but some is new or at least only lightly discussed elsewhere. The main objective of this book was to organize contemporary ICT security information in a manner that makes it most applicable to the security and assurance challenges developing due to IP convergence.

Index

Analog to Digital Converters (ADCs), 116
assessment paradigm, 62, 138
Asynchronous Transfer Mode (ATM), 166
ATM. *See* Asynchronous Transfer Mode

BGP. *See* Border Gateway Protocol
Blue Sky convergence, 9, 17
Border Gateway Protocol (BGP), 16, 253
British Columbia Institute of Technology (BCIT), 115
business continuity (BC) capabilities, 16

cable deployment, 188
Capability Maturity Model for Software (CMM-SW), 222
Capability Maturity Model Integration (CMMI), 222
CIRTs. *See* Computer Incident Response Teams
Committee of Sponsoring Organizations of the Treadway Commission (COSO), 36, 47
Communication Assistance to Law Enforcement Agencies (CALEA), 81
Computer and Information Science and Engineering (CISE), 262
Computer Incident Response Teams (CIRTs), 180, 194
converged sensitivity, 29
understanding phenomena of, 35

convergence 101, 7
Blue Sky, 9, 17
conflicting priorities of, 21–25
market, 12–14
regulatory drivers of, 19–20
taxonomy of, 8–9
transparent, 9
triple play, 9
competitive driver, 18
cost driver, 15–17
customer-centric routing, 141

DCS. *See* Distributed control system
descriptive techniques
control and safeguard worksheets, 136–137
risk worksheets, 58–59
de-standardization process, 19
Digital Rights Management (DRM), 113–115, 143
Digital to Analog Converters (DACs), 116
disaster recovery (DR) capabilities, 16
distributed control system (DCS), 14
Distributed Denial of Service (DDoS), 55
DRM. *See* Digital rights management

electrical environment sensitivity, 103–106, 183–184
detection safeguards, 189
prevention safeguards, 185–188
electromagnetic compatibility (EMC), 104